Soul-Centered Leadership

Soul-Centered Leadership

R. Michael Anderson, M.B.A., M.A.

Executive Joy! Publishing
SAN DIEGO, CALIFORNIA

Soul-Centered Leadership

R. Michael Anderson
Executive Joy! Publishing
PO Box 381
Camdenton, MO 65020, USA

www.executivejoy.com
www.soul-centered-leadership.com
info@executivejoy.com

Ordering Information:
Quantity sales. Special discounts are available on quantity purchases by corporations, associations, and others. For details, contact us at info@executivejoy.com.

Soul-Centered Leadership/ R. Michael Anderson. —1st ed.
ISBN 978-0-9906605-1-4

Contents

My Story

April 1st, 2008, was a hell of a day for me.

I was sitting on my sofa rolling a joint. I had the Johnny Walker poured and was about to snort some cocaine. That was the way I dealt with problems back then. And this particular day certainly had its fill of problems.

At the time, I owned three software businesses. I was the CEO of two of them, and in my largest one, my business partner and I were not getting along. I had started the business myself three years earlier and brought him on after the first year to run the operations, offering him a small share of equity (ownership). We'd had incredible growth during that initial run and I wanted to keep growing—fast.

My partner was more conservative. He saw the massive payroll every month and felt the pressure of adding new people, offices, and further growth. In addition, he kept asking for more equity. On two previous occasions I had given it to him and then he came and asked again.

I finally told him no, that he had to stick to our agreement. He didn't take that well.

This brought a lot of tension in the office because we were at a standoff. He wanted more, and I wasn't going to give it to him. And every day the business got bigger and more complex. That plus the seventy-hour weeks we'd been working for the past couple of years combined to form a powder keg ready to explode.

April 1st it did.

I had just hung up the phone after talking with my divorce lawyer—yes, on top of it all, I was going through a divorce—and my business partner came to the door to ask a question about one of our customers. I gave him an answer which, as it turned out, wasn't the way he thought the matter should be handled. Our minor disagreement quickly escalated into a full-blown argument, complete with him shouting at me.

Have you ever seen someone so angry that they turn red, shake, and yell at the top of their lungs?

That was him.

I said, "Look, you're getting out of hand, and there are employees around. Go back to your office and let's talk about this after work."

He glared at me, stepped away in the direction of his office, and then appeared back in my doorway. His voice sounded different—it had become quieter, but held a sharper edge. He said, "I'm going to wipe that smile off of your face."

I thought, *Am I smiling? I don't think so . . .* I certainly didn't *feel* like smiling.

Then he came into my office, walked around my desk to where I was sitting, cocked his arm back, and hit me.

I saw it coming and turned, so the blow just glanced off of me. I stared at him, shocked. I don't think I was even angry at that moment. It was 10 in the morning and my business partner had just assaulted me. It was too much to take in.

As for him, he stood there a moment longer, glaring and furious, then stormed out

It took a little while for the shock to burn off. Nothing like that had ever happened to me before, nor could I ever have imagined it would. I sat there, asking myself *Did that just really happen? What do I do now?*

My mind was racing and I couldn't think straight. I ended up calling some friends who said that if it had happened once, it would probably happen again. So I went to the police station to report it. I filed a restraining order against him and then a lawsuit to dissolve the partnership. I also terminated him, which was my right as the majority owner in the company.

My life was falling apart. The divorce-which of course is a story within itself-was destroying my personal life. And now my business was in shambles. I felt like a failure.

By many outside markers, I was doing great on the "scoreboard" of life. On the material level I was "winning." My resume, what I had accomplished, was impressive. By this point in my life I had played semi-professional basketball in Europe, founded three international software companies, and even hung out at the Playboy mansion. I had set, and for the most part, achieved audacious goals.

I made lots of money. I partied all over the world.

From the outside it looked like my life was great.

Inside my life was a mess. I felt *zero* joy and fulfillment. I was incredibly hard on myself, always beating myself up. I couldn't understand why. Despite my success, I still felt driven to achieve what I was "supposed" to achieve. Even though I was *doing it*, succeeding more than most any others, the finish line seemed to be slipping further and further into the distance.

On the outside I was aggressive, insulting, and brash. I chased what I thought would be a "better" life, with more money and greater power, working harder, stepping on more people. On the inside I was scared, confused, and frustrated; all of which I really didn't admit to myself. I knew something was missing in my life, but I didn't know what it was.

It was easy to escape through alcohol and drugs. And when I say drugs, I mean the hard ones. Rather than asking myself the difficult questions about what was going on inside me, I shut myself down, disconnecting from reality because I just didn't know how to deal with reality at the time.

That's why that evening found me on my sofa with coke, booze, and weed as my companions of choice. If I couldn't process a divorce and an upheaval at my company, I could at least hide from the stress and pain and fear for a little while.

But something else happened. I had enough.

For some reason, joint in hand, I paused in my outer activity and paid attention to what was going inside me. I started to *reflect* on my life, because it sure wasn't going as planned. The first thing I became aware of was a profound feeling of emptiness, quickly followed by a wave of sadness, bordering on despair.

The emotions took shape as thoughts: *What is* wrong *with me? I'm a doer. An achiever. Why can't I achieve what I really want? And what* do *I really want?*

The answer came more quickly than I would've imagined possible, as if it had been waiting to be asked:

Peace. Contentment. Self-acceptance. Joy. That's what I really want.

And once I started this process of inner examination, it took on a life of its own. The thoughts rolled in: *I should have all of these things. I make it* look *like I do on the outside. But I really don't. Am I broken? Is there something wrong with me?*

Thoughts of the divorce, the assault, and a host of other "wrongs" flooded my mind. What was going on? Was I cursed? It wasn't fair. I got angry, first at myself, then at God. And I didn't even really believe in God! Why were other people happy and not me?

No wonder I'd been reluctant to look inside myself.

But then, out of nowhere I began to sense something *else* inside me.

Peacefulness. Quiet. Where had *they* come from? And why now?

The feelings didn't suppress or mute my sense of anger and helplessness; rather they seemed to swell up from somewhere within me and my perspective started to shift *away* from the negativity.

Something changed within me. Actually, to be more specific: *I* changed.

I realized simply that I needed to do things differently. I've always been proud of my ability to motivate myself and achieve goals. In that moment, it struck me: *I'm asking the wrong questions. I have the wrong goals.*

Right then I made two life-changing decisions. Instead of drinking and doing drugs, I went for a jog. I chose to do something to bring me *up* instead of *down.* My other decision? I would do whatever it took to get happy. *If I'm so good at achieving goals,* I thought, *why don't I make it my* goal *to become fulfilled?*

True Transformation

That led me down a path of searching. Fast-forward a few months and I found myself at a place I believe is one of the best on the planet to find this joy and fulfillment: The University of Santa Monica, where I ended up earning a Master's Degree in Spiritual Psychology.

The program had such a tremendous impact on me that after the Masters I went back for an additional two years of school. One of these programs was called Consciousness, Health, and Healing, which teaches deep spiritual practices. The second was Soul-Centered Coaching. I'm honored to say that I'm one of only 180 certified Soul-Centered Coaches on the planet.

I don't throw the word "transformational" around a lot, but I can honestly say that the entire experience transformed my life. Like a 180-degree transformation.

I used to be the guy who made a lot of money and wanted to show off how cool he was. My insecurity made me aggressive, and I was always on the attack. The strange thing is that it was a mask; inside I felt like a fraud and I was afraid someone would find out.

Now there's a whole new me. It's as if I've woken up from a bad dream. Life is easier. I'm kinder with myself and others. People comment on my warmth and vulnerability. I have a warm, inviting presence, and I connect to others with ease.

I say this with a sense of humility and surprise as well as pride. In a way, I can take some credit for this transformation, as it took a lot of work and more courage than anything else in my life. But really it was due to something bigger than the "me." Connecting with that greater sense of self and the universe is what this book is about. On one hand, my journey is particular to me, but on the other it's representative of a journey all of us can take in life—a journey I believe we must take to find happiness, joy, inner peace, and fulfillment.

I did follow through on that goal I set myself in 2008, sitting alone on my coach, when I saw the choice between continuing to escape my life through drugs and alcohol and taking charge of it. I chose taking personal ownership, and the difference in who I am between then and now is like night and day.

Convergence

It gradually dawned on me that I was used to thinking there were two of me: the kind, loving, compassionate guy at home, and the hard-core, driven me at work. So during my process of transformation, one thing I asked myself was this; Why do they have to be separate?

When we go about it in the most holistic way, when we integrate the kind, loving, compassionate person into the workplace, we don't reduce our effectiveness; we experience greater power.

Power to make change in our lives, in our businesses, and in our relationships.

When you bring your heart and soul into your leadership, you affect employees, customers, suppliers, partners, the community, the environment, and more. The energy you bring to work, how you show up each day has a huge impact. The more positive the energy, the more enriching and affirming the change you can bring about.

Haven't you ever wondered, how can I do more?

Many of us make our positive mark in the world through creating and business. This gives us the influence to bring more goodness into the world. When I started to use these skills in my business life, our growth took off. I pivoted the purposes of my businesses to do the right things, to impact all of my stakeholders in a positive way, and success seemed to naturally follow. In 2013 I was named San Diego Social Entrepreneur of the Year and one of my companies, Radiant Technologies, received the #1 Best Place to Work award in San Diego.

I've written Soul-Centered Leadership to share the skills that will help you effect transformative change in your life and business. Through my speaking and educating, I've seen these tools change and elevate countless individuals—whether they were better or worse off than I was on that dark night of April 1, 2008.

This stuff works. It did for me.

Now let's make it work for you.

How to Use This Book

I'm going to be very straightforward here; you might not need to read this whole book.

If you've done a lot of personal development work or have studied psychology and want to get to the really deep stuff, then you can either skip or browse the first two parts. I would focus on Self-Limiting Beliefs onwards. I say this because I do start with some fundamentals and I don't want you to give up before you get to the ultra-powerful skills that are in the third part.

So you have complete freedom to skip or skim anything you would like (not that you need my permission for that anyway!).

One piece of feedback I received from readers of an early draft of this book was that it there's a lot here. That's true. There's a lot offered up in a relatively short space. Each chapter could be dramatically expanded; in fact, someone could write a separate book on each individual one (and many in fact have).

I've written this book with business leaders in mind, the achievers of the world, and those aspiring leaders who are on the way to join their ranks. This doesn't mean you have to be a leader to appreciate and benefit from the book. I believe all of us have leadership potential, and besides this, the exercises in these pages can help anyone create greater success. But achievers tend to process information very quickly. We find what we need, absorb it, and adapt it to our needs. This is what I've taken into account in the writing of this book.

Your time is valuable, so this book goes quickly. For each skill, we'll get right to the point, give an example, and then learn how to implement it. Then we'll move on to the next one.

In Real Life

Chapters in Parts II and III (and some in Part I) have an In Real Life section at the end. These are bullet point briefs showing how you can immediately integrate what you've learned in the chapter into your life. These sections also show you where the material fits in in actual business situations.

Exercises / Membership Site

Almost every chapter in Parts II and III has exercises associated with it. The exercises are longer, multi-step processes that will enable you to work on a deeper level to effect greater change in your life. You will be able to access these through an online membership site that also provides bonus videos and audios to supplement the book.

All of the exercises are printable from the membership site and I encourage you to work through them with paper and pen/pencil in hand, rather than typing. It's been demonstrated that doing so is more effective in processes such as these. You can also order a workbook with all the exercises in it by going to http://tiny.cc/scl-workbook.

To get your login and password from the membership site (again it's free) go to http://tiny.cc/scl-member.

Proper Mindset

The number one way to get the most out of this book is with the proper mindset.

As you read, keep an open mind. Find out where things work for you, rather than don't work. This book is about engaging with life and leadership and your true self—not finding out what's "wrong" with you and how to fix it. Explore these ideas—and through them, yourself—and experiment with ways to adapt them to your life.

Soul-Centered Leadership is a combination of emotional intelligence, psychology, and a general type of spirituality. If you follow a particular religious belief system/practice, you have one of two choices as you read this book.

You can try to think of all the ways the techniques here don't match your religious beliefs...Or you can see how the information does match your beliefs.

Don't focus on the problems, focus on the solutions. The same goes if I bring up a topic you've had exposure to before. Try not to think of all the ways my approach differs from yours or another author's. Just read it through and see if it fits for you from this new angle. Consider, too, that a perspective that's different from your own doesn't have to negate yours; perhaps, in fact, it can enhance and expand it.

That's why I keep searching myself, to find those different ways of looking at things that help me grow.

Your inner world determines your outer reality. If you look for reasons why you can't integrate these principles into your life, you'll find them. But if you see what works, your journey will be underway.

What Lies Ahead

Part I – The Fundamentals

In Part I I'll share the basic emotional intelligence and spiritual concepts that form the building blocks for the rest of the book. This is the foundation of your practice. There's not a lot about business or leadership in this part; it's here to make sure you have the right information moving forward.

Part II – Essential Principles

In Part II you'll learn more specific principles to connect the mainly psychological concepts to specific scenarios in your life. These principles become part of a toolkit to use in different parts of your life. You'll also start to see how you can affect people and the world as a Soul-Centered Leader.

Part III – Life Integration Skills

In Part III you'll learn life-integration skills, many based on spiritual principles. You'll learn how to use the toolkit in a more holistic fashion and gain profound new perspectives on how to live and lead.

Part IV – The Soul-Centered Leadership System

Part IV lays out a system you can easily utilize in your own life when issues come up. By this point you'll have learned many tools and ways to implement them, and the system in Part IV offers an easy way to remember and apply them in different situations.

As you progress through the book the material you're learning will increase exponentially. Principles, skills, and tools build on each other and become more powerful the more frequently you utilize them and the deeper you go with them. You will begin to see a synergistic effect as the tools become a part of you through your continued practice. Keep this in mind as you make your way through the book.

Continue Your Training Online

As a companion to the book, go online and join a free 90-minute Virtual Training called ***3 Secrets to Transforming from Boss to Leader.***

In a short period of time you can learn some fast actionable strategies to motivate and inspire your team, shift your career into high gear and build something great.

Just go to http://tiny.cc/scl-course and sign-up now.

This Book's Purpose

My personal mission in life is to raise the consciousness of the world by elevating leaders. While this book is a step towards that, the true intention of this book is not to just present information; it's to have you integrate what I present here into your every life. To do that you need to start a regular practice.

I was talking to a woman who wanted to make changes in her life. She said "I do a lot of self-improvement."

I asked, "What do you mean by that?"

"Well, I watch a lot of videos on the internet."

I nodded. "Yes, but what do you do to move yourself forward?" She looked perplexed, so I explained to her that watching videos isn't doing. You need to do work to change your beliefs, patterns, and ultimately results. For example, if a book contains exercises, you need to do them or you're just inputting data into your brain. We get more data and information than we know what to do with dumped into us on a daily basis, simply by turning on our computers and surfing the web. But data rarely means anything until you put it to work.

That's why author Byron Katie calls her system *The Work*. Because unless you do the work, nothing is going to change.

If you want to pick up a new sport, reading a book about it, watching YouTube videos, or even going to a weekend workshop wouldn't get you very far. You may learn about it, maybe even get a little hands-on experience, but your skill level won't significantly change with that small amount of effort. Mastering a sport—mastering anything—takes practice over an extended period of time.

That's why, in addition to this book I am also offering you, at no charge, a community that takes the form of a private Facebook group. It's a safe and impactful way to connect and grow with other people that have the same intentions as you. Working together we can all deepen in our practice of being a Soul-Centered Leader. I'm there too, both to keep up my own practice and to serve and assist you in your own journey. The community will offer support, methods for developing your practice, and a variety of ways to integrate this material into your life.

Sure, you can read this book, and I can pretty much guarantee that what you find in these pages will empower you to make significant change in your life. But to take it to another level you need to do the exercises, and the community will provide a support system for you.

Go to the link http://tiny.cc/scl-member to access the membership site (explained below) and join the community.

Introduction

This book takes you on a journey of integration.

Using what you'll learn in these pages, you will infuse every aspect of your life with the power of your spiritual beliefs. Whether you call your higher power God, Allah, Buddha, Jesus, Jehovah, spirit, the universe or something else, the principles in this book will bring you closer to your source. They will guide you to draw on your innermost power and use it to do amazing things in this world.

(As a side note, I will use the phrases higher power and the universe to cover what you may call God, Allah, Buddha, Jesus, Jehovah, spirit, or whatever word or phrase you choose to use. Just know that when I use those terms, them are meant to be universal and inclusive to whatever you believe.)

Since you are reading this book, I'm sure you have at least some idea of what your spiritual beliefs are. You might have formed them through participating in a religion, through various life experiences and teachers—or you may simply have an inner knowing that we are all connected in some way. And I imagine that your relationship with your higher power gives you strength, faith, and confidence, and that it brings out a better you.

Wouldn't it be amazing if you could take that same power and deeply integrate it into your everyday work life, in service to creating greatness in this world?

Leadership is a constantly evolving area of study and practice, and there have been great advances in understanding it in the recent past. Now more than ever, leaders show up authentically, guided by ethics and values, truly caring about more than just dividends and investors. People are using their leadership skills to create better lives for all their stakeholders.

Now there's a new way of leading, one that originates from the deepest level possible within you, the part that serves as the conduit between you and your higher power: Your soul. That's what this book is about. Soul-Centered Leadership.

It's about integrating the most powerful forces in the universe—your spirituality, your higher power, your love—and giving you a system to live every minute as a channel for the divine. You may have had glimpses of what such a way of living looks and feels like. I'm sure you're engaging bits and pieces of it now, whether you realize it or not.

There's a level of being and doing in Soul-Centered Leadership that is unlocked with courage and faith. Once you become aware of how to incorporate these principles consciously, you will find a new dimension of fulfillment and success in life. The payoffs are massive.

What Soul-Centered Leadership Looks Like

Consider this vision of your life:

You have an unwavering source of knowledge and confidence within yourself that functions as both a guide and a toolset. As you accept this power within yourself you'll stop ever feeling like a fraud, you don't belong, or that something is wrong with you. As you unlock your inner natural leader, your old fears and uncertainties will fall away. You'll find that doing the right thing for yourself and others becomes natural, and you no longer have to compromise your ethics to make money or create a successful business.

You'll overcome those pervasive feelings of uneasiness, of not-belonging. You'll move forward and leave your stress, anxiety, and ADD (Attention Deficit Disorder) tendencies behind. Perhaps for the first time ever, you will become truly comfortable in your own skin.

You finally discover your purpose. In fact, you'll receive crystal clarity about what you stand for and will easily express it. Leadership—and life in general—will become effortless and flowing.

As a kind of side effect, you'll find that you're more likeable. People trust you more. Many start following your lead based simply on your powerful presence and energy. You discover new depths of patience and find you can listen and connect with others on a deep level.

Things you have always wanted to do seem to start happening almost of their own accord. Business and personal growth, smoother relationships, health—everything starts coming together.

Things start going better physically, too. You start sleeping more, eating better, living healthier; all without much effort.

It'll be like you've stepped into a whole new life, one where you have a sense of peace and contentment, no matter what happens around you. And from this base you'll finally start creating on a grand scale, tapping into a power you never knew you had.

It's like you've got super powers; which, in a way, you do. And the world is a much better place because of it.

All of this, and more, is closer than you think.

Welcome to the journey of Soul-Centered Leadership.

Part I - The Fundamentals

Part I, the shortest of all the main sections, is an overview of basic emotional intelligence and spiritual concepts.

There's a challenge in presenting these ideas, as some people have a lot of exposure to them while others (like me just 10 short years ago) have none. Of course, even if you do find some of these ideas familiar, what we'll be discussing could really be studied for a lifetime without exhausting its meaning and potential.

That said, you will be getting the short and sweet version of these ideas in Part I. If you have questions or want to understand more about a particular concept, visit the Soul-Centered Leadership community to ask me directly.

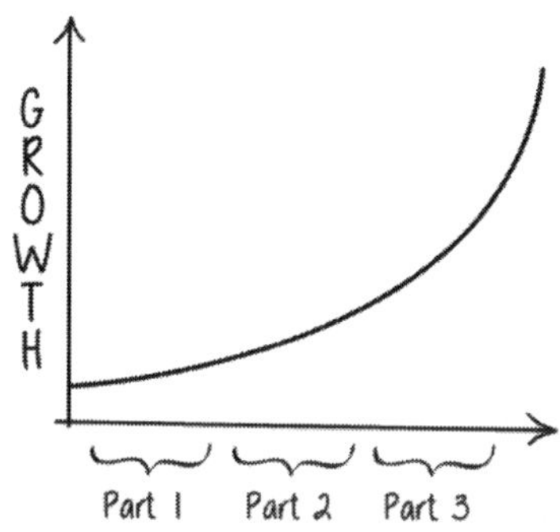

Ready to get started? Buckle up and read on. It's going to be a great trip.

The "Soul" in Soul-Centered Leadership

Before defining precisely what Soul-Centered Leadership is, let's start with defining what a soul is.

It's a difficult question in its own right, because a soul defies definition. You can't see a soul. There's no scientific proof it exists and no evidence strong enough to make an open and shut case for it. What's more, even the great spiritual traditions of the world that accept the existence of a soul don't all agree on a definition for it.

But consider the following:

- Have you ever had a sense of déjà vu when, say, you arrived somewhere new and were sure you'd been there before?
- Have you ever felt instantly connected to someone?
- Have you ever had something so random happen to you at exactly the right time that it's just about statistically impossible?
- Have you ever felt compelled to do something that seemed illogical, yet done it, and had it turn out wonderfully?
- Have you read about near-death experiences and discovered how everyone tells basically the same story upon their "return?'

These are all flashpoints of the soul at work. They remind us that the universe is considerably more complicated, rich and mysterious than we're used to thinking it is. By extension, so are we. The peculiar moments described above—and there are many other examples in human experience—are moments when something within us connects with the wider universe.

The soul, then, is our conduit to something more. The soul is you, but it's a bigger you than you're consciously aware of much of the time. The soul is our connection to our higher power. You might find your own spiritual path leads through Judaism, Christianity, Islam, Buddhism or any number of other sacred traditions. You might just have a general sense that we are all connected. The practice of Soul-Centered Leadership isn't based on any specific belief, but it taps into the fact that there is something beyond just what is visible, that there is something more—to us and to the universe at large—than meets the eye.

The soul is what makes us aware of this. And when we are "soul-centered" we are acting in sync with the universe. When we do this, when we create in line with our higher power, we are capable of more amazing things than we've ever dreamed possible.

Think about it this way: many people think that their higher power is the creator of the universe. If we are made in the image of that higher power, then our true nature is to create. "Creation" means many things. We create relationships, family, community, inventions, and businesses. Really, we create our lives.

Conscious evolution is you becoming more centered in listening to what your higher power is saying, and acting on that information. It's a process of receiving that information and moving forward with it.

This book teaches you specific skills to create through the soul. While it's a business book written primarily for managers, executives, and owners, leadership and creation shows up in many different areas, and everyone can benefit from developing their own inherent abilities to lead.

Based on my beliefs and experience, the higher power in our lives—as well as our souls—are manifestations of love and compassion. Following this way of thinking means that embracing love and compassion leads to the most powerful type of creation available.

Soul-Centered Leadership involves connecting to your higher power and co-creating along with that all-powerful, loving, creative force.

The Relationship with Yourself

This book only focuses on one relationship, and it's the most important one you have: your relationship with yourself. That's because this relationship mirrors every other relationship in your life. What this means in the bigger picture is that as you come into a more loving, compassionate, accepting relationship with yourself, your relationship with your co-workers, your family, your career, and your health will improve.

Think about the times when things were going well for you. Didn't it seem like everyone around you was much nicer? And you got along with them better? When you're going through a tough time, it's often the opposite. People get on your nerves more and life in general becomes more difficult.

In psychology, this is called a projection. It happens in all areas of life. What we see on the outside mirrors how we feel on the inside.

Here are a few examples where projection might show up.

If you have resistance around taking risks and have a belief that you are holding yourself back, you may resent people who you believe are risk takers. You may even talk about them negatively or try to bring them down.

If you are good at something, like sales or entrepreneurship, you might think that everyone else has those same skills; if they don't, you hold it against them.

If you dislike someone else, you may convince yourself that they dislike you.

If you are unhappy with your appearance, you may gossip about someone else's appearance; maybe they are too fat, or too ugly, or even too beautiful.

By looking at what your beliefs about others are, you can often trace them back to how you feel about yourself. When you take the next step and heal those negative feelings about yourself, you come into a better relationship with yourself and others. In fact, if you are comfortable in your own skin, you are more likely to feel inclined to serve others rather than judge them.

The Ego and Authentic Self

Let's break down our understanding of consciousness into two aspects: The Ego and the Authentic Self.

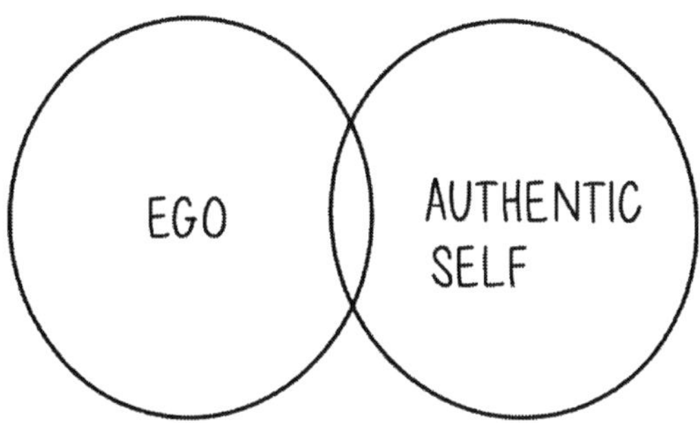

You can think of the Authentic Self as your soul. It comes from a place of pure love.

The ego, on the other hand, is only concerned about three things: comfort, control, and security. It resists change. It doesn't like to be vulnerable. It always wants you to look perfect. Because of these characteristics, the ego can get a bad rap. But it's a very necessary part of your functioning. It's what drives you forward. It's your "doer."

The problem is that you can get too ego-focused. When the ego alone drives you, your goal becomes winning at all costs. Ego by itself is all about making more money, protecting your image, and gaining power. The ego is scared to ever let go of control. The end result is that you end up tripping over your own feet, thinking you have to do everything on your own, that you have no other reserves to call on.

But this isn't true: we have our Authentic Self, our soul, which keeps us connected to an unimaginably vast source of power and love. When we let this drive us, our ego can take its proper place and we move forward as one.

> ***You are at your most powerful when you are guided by the Authentic Self, a place of love, and have the ego work in service to that.***

Neale Donald Walsch, in his book *Conversations with God*, talks about the *sponsoring thought*, which is either love or fear. This means that every single thought, action, or emotion you have can be traced back to a sponsoring thought of love or fear.

Love comes from the Authentic Self; fear comes from the ego.

Look at your goals. Which ones of them are ego-based? What projects are you embarking on in your life because you "have to" or "should"? Those are the ones being put forward by the ego. They're based in fear. The same thing with your drive to achieve success, often at all costs. Where's that coming from? In most instances, that's coming from the ego too.

That's okay. It was for me not all that long ago. I had to ask myself: What was I afraid of? Where was my fear coming from? The answers were clear: I was afraid of not being "enough." Not being worthy. Not being accepted.

Any of that sound familiar?

Of course, there was more to life than that. There was excitement and enthusiasm, even growth along the way. I experienced the joy of being in the game and using my skills to engage with the world. And I did create and do some very good things.

But behind that was the fear. Fear that I always needed to prove myself in order to "be" something or someone. And that was my ego, pulling the strings behind the show, maintaining control.

The interesting thing is that when you're a leader driven by your ego, you attract others driven by their egos. The funny thing is that these people are the ones that try the hardest to act like they never have fear.

It can happen even when you're acting in pursuit of noble causes. Have you ever met someone who's working for a cause and who just spews negativity? Often it's the hatred of something or someone that's driving them. You get the sense that they're not in it to help; they're in it to punish someone or something else. Maybe they started out with the best of intentions, but at a certain point the ego stepped in to run the show. It's a good reminder that even if you're fighting the good fight, your ego can commandeer your emotional compass and ramp up your sense of self-righteousness.

Self Esteem and Confidence

Basically by definition, leadership is difficult. Think about it—normally you start with one set of duties and a certain level of responsibility. Then you take a risk, like starting your own business, or convince someone to promote you, and you get a whole new list of duties and a ton more responsibility, often with no real training or support—and everyone is watching to see how well you do.

That pressure will often lead you to slip into fear and ego-based thinking. You may have a feeling that expectations are too high, that you weren't up to the task, or now that you've climbed higher you've got a longer way to fall.

It takes a strong sense of self to not go into those behaviors. Poor leadership is often a result of lack of confidence. It can lead to micromanaging, lack of trust and transparency, talking down to people and poor communication. Without appropriate self-esteem, leaders are in the unfortunate position of having a job to do but not having the inner tools to excel—or possibly even succeed—at it.

The alternative to that, of course, is that as you grow as a leader you evolve as a human being at the same time. Much of this work in Soul-Centered Leadership will infuse you with a true sense of confidence. Not the kind born out of arrogance; but rather the quiet, inner confidence that comes from the fact that you know you are whole and complete just as you are now.

Nothing needs to be done to make you a worthy person. You already are one; you just have to bring that knowledge to the surface and live it. That's what this book will help you do.

5 Levels of Consciousness

At the University of Santa Monica, they teach a helpful way of looking at consciousness called the "five-line" model[1]. It's based on five levels of consciousness: the physical, mental, emotional, unconscious and, at the deepest level, the Authentic Self—which is your essence, and which is made up of true love and compassion.

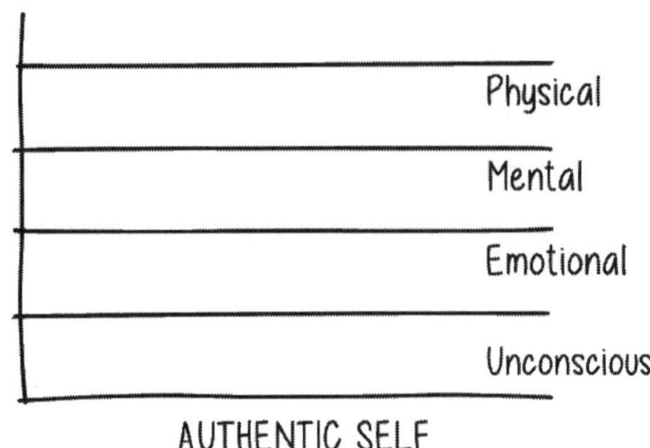

When the Authentic Self expresses itself from your deepest level of being, that specific expression must work its way through the levels above it before reaching "surface" consciousness, where you are aware of it as part of your everyday thoughts and feelings. If you have unresolved issues at any level along the way, the expression from the Authentic Self gets distorted. This in turn results in unhealthy and contradictory behaviors, disease, and addictions, and it can wreak havoc with everything you're trying to improve in your life.

Because of this, when you're healthy and clean in the upper four levels—physical, mental, emotional, and unconscious —you are much more connected to your Authentic Self. There's simply less clutter in the way. Let's look at an example.

Imagine that your Authentic Self, from the very core of your being, expresses the idea of self-love. This natural feeling bubbles up from within you, but as it rises it encounters an unconscious belief that you aren't attractive. Now this latter belief carries an emotional

[1] Here's a great video of Dr. Ron Hulnick explaining the five-line model: https://www.youtube.com/watch?v=D9BTLVE6TJM.

charge of depression. As if from nowhere you start to experience thoughts (at the mental level of consciousness) of not being good enough. Finally, at the physical level you reach for a sugary treat to distract yourself, or overeat in general and end up carrying extra weight to suppress your negative emotions and thoughts. You may sabotage your physical beauty, doing things like dressing and acting in an unattractive way. The end result of this process is that you've reacted to the prompts of your subconscious, emotional, mental and physical levels of consciousness, but the original message—that you, as an Authentic Self, are perfect as you are—has been distorted almost beyond recognition.

Now let's say that you recognize something is wrong. At the very least, your extra weight and depression spur the desire to change. But if you only focus on one or two or even three of the levels of consciousness, your changes won't take.

For example, let's say you start to make a change on the physical level: you alter your diet and lose some weight. But if you don't address the mental, emotional, and unconscious reasons for why you were overweight in the first place (depression and a feeling of being unattractive), one of two things will likely happen: either you'll gain the weight back, or the reason you were keeping the weight on will manifest as some other issue in your life to be dealt with. Maybe you'll get sick or take on another addiction.

In other words, in order to address the real problems in your life you must clear the path to your Authentic Self so its messages can get through in their original form. Soul-Centered Leadership then, in a way, focuses on eliminating what is blocking you from your Authentic Self and your authentic expression.

The Ego's Resistance

Be warned: once you begin the process of change, your ego won't necessarily like it. In fact, it's to be expected that your ego will resist your evolution.

The ego doesn't like change. Its goal is comfort, control, and security, and these are all based on the fear of change. It wants things to stay exactly the way they are in order to have control and thereby safety. Especially when it comes to learning material such as this, your ego might stop you short and convince you you've already learned all you need to know and you don't need any more conscious evolution. Or it might try planting seeds of doubt, whispering that it's not working . . . and it would be so much easier to just stop. Or it'll try to be practical and inform you that you don't just have time for making changes. The ego is a master of Self sabotage.

Don't underestimate the ego—that little bugger is crafty! It's got a job to do and it takes it very seriously.

Throughout the process of becoming a Soul-Centered Leader you'll work on all the different levels of awareness, though the exercises in this book often specifically address the emotional and unconscious levels. These take more work and directed effort to change—but that's where the real gold lies.

In Real Life

What actions have you taken in the past that you regret, or that you feel have held you back in life?

Reflect on how they may have been caused by lack of confidence and ego-based behavior, and how a new approach would better serve you and others involved. For ease of understanding, consider focusing on one or two behaviors to get you started with this exercise.

Access the exercises through the membership site at
http://tiny.cc/scl-member

Self-Leadership

There are several techniques that are used to manage and lead yourself—prerequisites to effectively leading others. They have to do with being aware of what's going on around and inside you, and then choosing a productive and elevated way forward.

The Illusion of Control

I used to be a master of control.

Or maybe I should say "slave." I spent so much of my time and energy trying to control everything that it took over my whole focus. In a way, this behavior served me well over the years. I thrived in sales and other business dealings when I went out of my way to control absolutely every variable I could. But the process was exhausting, and it drove me—and others in my life—crazy.

This is why one of my greatest lessons turned out to be that there's really only one thing I can control: myself.

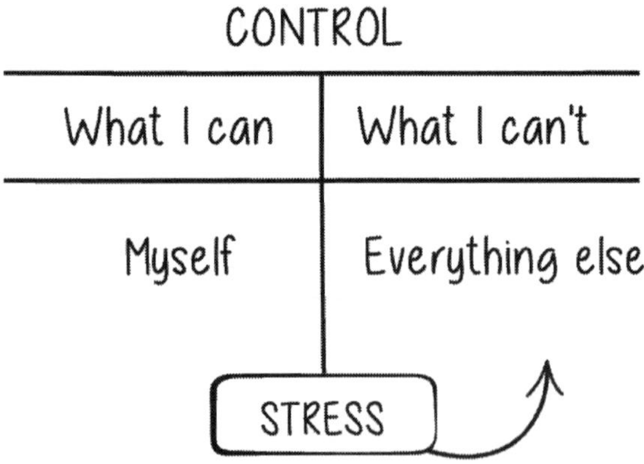

Think about it: how much energy do you spend trying to control other people, situations, outcomes?

Let's differentiate between "influencing" and "controlling." Can a salesperson control whether they make their quota for the period? No. They can influence the process by doing many things; making prospecting calls, getting coaching from their sales manager, spending time learning product information that could bolster sales, and so on. But at the end of the day they can't directly control the number of sales they make. Their actions may influence the count but there will always be circumstances beyond their control that make it impossible to dictate exactly their sales rate.

To illustrate this, let me take you back to before I started my own companies. I held an US based sales director position for a global software company. I always had success in software sales and most of the time made my quota. In 2011 things were on track until the 9/11 terrorist attacks, at which point not one of us in our company made quota. Of course what happened that fateful day was out of my control, yet it did affect my business goals.

This of course doesn't mean you keep salespeople that don't make their quota. However if someone is underperforming, what you should do is see if they are doing all the tasks under their control correctly. If they are, and they still aren't being successful, then they are wrong for that position.

The message is to focus on what you can control. Doing otherwise is futile, and it actually takes your energy away. This doesn't just apply to sales. When you apply this idea to your own life you can see it's a central concept for improving effectiveness, personal evolution, and downright sanity.

It's so fundamental that we will drill down on it more in the next few chapters.

Reaction versus Response

When something happens, there are two ways you can go: you can react or respond. The differences are subtle yet powerful.

A reaction is the course you instinctually take. There's no real thought or choice being made; you just go forward with what comes up. You stub your toe, you swear. Someone cuts you off in traffic, you slam on the horn and maybe give a one-finger salute. Someone shouts at you, you shout back. The issue with some reactions, especially when in stressful situations, is that they can lead to undesirable consequences. Anger, resentment, and defensiveness all are outcomes of being reactive. As a leader you have to be particularly careful, as people are extremely tuned in to your actions. Gossiping, talking down to people, offending someone, yelling, passive aggressiveness and so on don't only make you a less effective leader, they also "trickle down" and negatively impact your employees, making them less effective as well.

A response, on the other hand, is something you choose. It's constructive and considered. When we respond we take stock of a situation and choose an action that moves things forward.

Here's a short example. Say you are leading a company and a salesperson lets you know that you lost a large customer.

What is your reaction? It's most likely anger. Mine would probably be the same. We are competitors! No one likes to lose a customer.

Then, because you are mindful, you realize that anger and upset won't get you anywhere. As a strong businessperson, you reflect on the situation and see how you can better respond to it.

First, you personally call the customer to see if you can get them back. If you can't, you see why they cancelled their contract. Then you call an all-company meeting to go over why you lost them so you never lose a customer like that again. Finally, you make it a rallying cry to your sales team to double the revenue you just lost from that client.

Which would help your company more at the end of the day, your reaction or your response?

By becoming aware of your reactions, and instead choosing a higher-level response, you take control of life, instead of having life take control of you.

Your Potential

There's a lot of vague information out there about living up to your potential. The general suggestion seems to be that that there is some invisible level of success you can reach, and if you aren't reaching it you're doing something wrong. If you focus on that, you'll drive yourself crazy.

I have another take on potential that inspires me to make better choices and reminds me to respond instead of react.

To live your potential, make the highest-level decision you can make – right now.

This mantra is focused on the present moment. It's not about what you did or didn't do in the past. It has nothing to do about the future. It's about now.

Some people ask me how they will know what their highest-level decision is. In this book you'll learn skills that will make that more clear. For right now, just trust that if you reflect on what is going on in your life and what seems to be coming from the true Authentic Self place, you will have a good answer. At the very least you will slow yourself down, away from "reaction" and closer to "response." In response mode you will broaden your vision to understand more of what's going on around you, and then incorporate that into your decision-making process.

A Soul-Centered Coach

John Wooden, the hall of fame UCLA college basketball coach who won 10 NCAA men's basketball championships in ten years, and who *The Sporting News* honored as the greatest coach in American sports history, never talked about winning. What he *did* talk about was; making the right pass, working hard, respecting your teammates, the competition, the game, yourself.

Famously, on the first day of practice, he would go over how to tie your shoes. His point? If you aren't doing the small things correctly, how are you going to do the big things correctly?

He never got down on his team for losing. Neither did he praise them for winning. Any given player, even the whole team, can influence the outcome of a game, but it can't actually control it. If players were lazy, made stupid decisions, or didn't concentrate, he let them know this wasn't acceptable. That was something they could change. By the same token, if they hustled, played as a team, and gave it their all, he was encouraging whether or not they won.

So, for example, if they won but hadn't been playing good defense and chasing after rebounds, they were in trouble. If they played their hearts out and lost, he would beam with pride.

Here's what Coach Wooden said at his TED talk in 2007:

> "You never heard me mention winning. Never mention winning. My idea is that you can lose when you outscore somebody in a game, and you can win when you're outscored...I used to say that when a game is over, and you see somebody that didn't know the outcome, I hope they couldn't tell by your actions whether you outscored an opponent or the opponent outscored you."
>
> TED. (2007, February) John Wooden: The difference between winning and succeeding. Retrieved from *https://www.ted.com/talks/john_wooden_on_the_difference_between_winning_and_success?language=en*

Sounds like Coach Wooden knew a thing or two about control. He applied all his focus to what was in his realm of what he and his team could change. And it worked out pretty well for him.

In Real Life

Where are you experiencing stress? What are you trying to control that's actually out of your control? How can you shift your focus onto what you can control?

Start becoming aware of these reactions;

- Defensiveness
- Anger
- Passive Aggressiveness (when someone does something you don't like, and you hold it against them, without confronting them)
- Anxiety
- Upset

Once you notice them, think about how you can live your potential in the moment. What's the highest level decision, based on love and compassion, you can make right now? If you can get into the habit of doing this whenever you need to make a decision of consequence, you will begin to quiet the storm of reactions most of us experience on a daily basis and which distracts us from our goals.

Access the exercises through the membership site at
http://tiny.cc/scl-member

Meditation

When I started the Spiritual Psychology course, most of my classmates had at least some background in emotional intelligence and consciousness.

Not me. I was starting at ground zero. The achiever in me figured I had to catch up, so I asked my classmates what I could do to speed up my evolution. The first one I asked said “meditation.” I didn’t like that answer, because my perception of meditation at the time was that it was “doing nothing,” and that it took too long a time to have an effect—if it ever even did.

There had to be a better, faster way, so I asked the same question of another classmate.

Their answer: “Meditation.”

Five people in a row gave me the same answer. So I stopped asking and started meditating.

Now when other people ask me the same question, my answer is also “meditation.” When people—entrepreneurs especially—hear that they get flustered and say, “I tried meditation before. It doesn’t work for me. My mind keeps chattering.”

That actually means it is working! If you have the awareness that your mind is chattering, then you are aware of your thoughts, and that is what meditation is for: having the focus and awareness of what’s going on inside you. There’s a reason that monks meditate silently for years and years on end. It gives them a new perspective on the world and connects them in new and amazing ways. The same can happen for you.

Some say praying is talking to your higher power, while meditating is listening to it. Personally, I get a whole lot more when I am listening rather than talking. And I’ve found my higher power is pretty smart! Some also say that the divine is in the silence. In the nothing. It’s in the time between breaths, the space between the atoms.

Meditation is how you bring that divine into your own life.

Improved Focus and Awareness

I meet and work with people who have a hard time focusing. They're so fidgety and distracted that they can barely hold a conversation. Classic ADD symptoms. What's more, because they have trouble communicating they encounter confusion at the office and home, and they often don't have very deep relationships because they are hard to connect with. Talking to them is like trying to hit a moving target.

I know of one CEO who had these traits and who brought in a coach to try to get them under control. The coach talked to the CFO of the company, who was frustrated with the CEO. Why? It turns out the CEO would get up in the middle of a conversation and simply leave the room. When the coach reflected this to the CEO, he expressed surprise at himself: he wasn't even aware he did that!

When I come across people like this—something far more common that you might think—I find that most of them eat horribly, drink sugary drinks and caffeine all day long, never exercise, and often binge drink and do drugs. They wonder why they can't concentrate on anything!

You can probably anticipate what this has to do with meditation. A study by John T. Mitchell at Duke showed that in just eight weeks, 63% of respondents engaged in "mindfulness meditation" showed a 30% decline in ADHD symptoms like inattention and hyperactive-impulses. No one in the control group of non-meditators showed any improvement.

For my own part, before I adjusted my lifestyle, my ADD was all over the place. I couldn't concentrate for more than a few seconds. I wouldn't make eye contact with anyone. I would interrupt and fidget all the time. I was like a caged animal. Now, the world has slowed down so much for me—giving me more time and space to make intelligent, proactive and creative decisions. Before I felt out of synch with the world; now I feel in the flow. People often tell me how I have a very calming presence—something they never would have said of me earlier in my life.

This is what a Soul-Centered Leader brings: a simple, calming, confident presence. Just by being there you'll start to change the mood.

In Real Life

Meditation is so important that I've created a three-video course to get you started on a solid practice. The first segment offers a very basic way to start; the others offer intermediate and advanced techniques to enrich your experience.

Go to the membership site to watch the videos and get started now.

Access the exercises through the membership site at http://tiny.cc/scl-member

Mindfulness

The reason we practice meditation is to experience mindfulness.

Mindfulness is a slowing down of the world so you can live in it in the way you want. It's achieved through stillness and quiet.

Do you know how that feeling when things seem to be going a hundred miles an hour and it's like you're on autopilot? Something will happen and you think, "How did I miss that? What was I thinking?" Have you ever experienced the disastrous results that can arise from being in that state of mind?

On the other hand, have you ever come back from a relaxing vacation with your mind so clear and relaxed that you could remember everything, understand people better, and feel connected with everything going on around you?

That's the difference between being not being mindful and mindfulness.

Maybe you've been around someone who always seems present and focused, yet also relaxed. They don't get ruffled easily. They don't say a lot, but when they do speak it often seems that they say the exact right thing at the exact right time.

That person has a great deal of mindfulness.

Various studies have shown that mindfulness increases your heath, decreases the effects of aging, increases memory, improves your immune system, and results in less depression, anxiety, stress and anger. Being more mindful also contributes to better relationships, better parenting ability, and greater compassion for yourself and others. And, of course, when you're more mindful, the racing thoughts of ADD/ADHD are better managed, and you feel more at peace. At the same time you're functioning at a higher level of efficiency.

To become mindful is to become more in touch with the world. You can see how everything fits together. Life slows down and you become part of its flow. From this state it's far easier to tap into your inner wisdom—and your Authentic Self—because you experience inner focus and clarity. What else happens? For one, your intuition functions better. Maybe you'll experience a new clarity about how to approach a prospect, handle an employee issue, or create a new marketing message. You can increase the frequency of—and your own level of trust in—these messages by becoming more mindful.

Answer the Right Question

Mindfulness means enhanced awareness. That clarity affords you the opportunity to expend significantly less energy yet achieve greater results.

Albert Einstein once said "If I had an hour to solve a problem and my life depended on the solution, I would spend the first 55 minutes determining the proper question to ask, for once I know the proper question, I can solve the problem in less than five minutes."

How many times have you known something was off in your life, but you didn't slow down enough to figure out what the real issue was? Oftentimes in such situations we'll address the symptoms rather than the underlying issues, and then things get even worse. To get out of this trip, keep in mind one thing: No one's ever become more mindful by doing more, by speeding up. Mindfulness is achieved through stillness and quiet.

Mindfulness is a quality that the Soul-Centered Leader brings to the table. It is the calm in the storm that Soul-Centered Leaders carry inside them, a quiet, sincere energy in times of crisis. Mindfulness is the gateway to the quiet confidence that Soul-Centered Leaders wear so well.

In Real Life

In addition to a meditation practice, where else can you slow down in your life? Here are some suggestions:

- When you have a free minute, instead of whipping out your phone and checking e-mail, Facebook, Twitter, the stock market, fantasy football, or the news, give yourself that minute to breathe and reconnect. Just become present for that short period of time. Relax and enjoy the stillness.
- When driving, rather than flipping the dial or hooking up your music player, listen to simply nothing.
- Give yourself some space just before sleeping and immediately after waking up in the morning. Charge your phone somewhere outside of your bedroom. Don't check it right before bed, and don't do so first thing when you wake up checking e-mail.
- The next time you are bored and stuck, like in a meeting or a presentation that has lost your attention, focus on who's speaking. See if you can catch their inhalations and exhalations. What else can you learn about them by really focusing?
- Reflect on your life and all the positive things in it. Take a moment to have gratitude for your life as a whole.
- Take a common object in your hand. Turn it over. Look at the colors, at what it's made of. See what you can find out about it that you've never noticed before.
- When eating alone, do it like the monks do: focus on eating in silence. Don't have the radio, TV, phone, or computer on. Take each bite slowly. Chew your food. Realize how all the flavors mix together. Keep in your mind that food is the fuel for your body, and that it will power you over the next few days.

Access the exercises through the membership site at http://tiny.cc/scl-member

Emotional and Spiritual Mastery

I used to have a goal. It was to be completely evolved, meaning that I would never have a negative emotion and always would act in the most spiritual way possible. Then after graduating with my Spiritual Psychology master's degree, reality set in.

What I was aiming for was impossible.

Upset, anger, sadness—these are all part of my journey. Even after all the work I've done, I will still experience them. There's no eliminating them completely. When I first realized this I was confused. After all, I'd invested an immense amount of time and money earning a degree with the expectation that I would somehow be "fixed." Some part of me thought that when my tenure at the University of Santa Monica ended I would begin a lifetime of bliss.

I smile when I think about that now. Not only is that ideal impossible, it's also not what our lives are for. Mastery in life is not about being perfect or "fixed," it's about living life from a learning and evolving point of view.

Emotional and spiritual mastery is having the awareness of all of your feelings, accepting them, and having compassion for yourself through it all.

We're all human. Everyone goes through ups and downs, no matter how much "work" we do on ourselves. Yes, with the right tools we may have fewer downs, and they may not be as dramatic, but they won't ever go away forever. So stop trying to be perfect. Accept yourself just the way you are. You don't want to avoid your negative thoughts and feelings; you simply want to acknowledge and accept them.

As you start accepting your negative feelings, you'll notice how much less frequently they show up, and how much more quickly they disappear. Really it's about your relationship with yourself and true self-acceptance. If you judge part of yourself, what kind of inner dialogue does that start?

Not a very supporting one.

It takes courage to be OK with thoughts and feelings that you want to avoid. Real courage. Sometimes it's easy, and sometimes it takes time and work. But remember that we will be building a deep, bedrock-level of self-esteem. Try to fast-forward for just a minute and imagine how your life will be when you can experience negative feelings and thoughts. Tell yourself that it's okay to be having them and be compassionate with yourself anyway. That's what inner confidence is; being able to handle anything that life throws at you.

In Real Life

What are your expectations for yourself in regards to this book and your conscious evolution? What is your image of yourself after you read this book, do all the exercises, and work a strong spiritual practice?

Instead of imagining yourself as a perfect person with no upset, picture a strong individual who meets life with acceptance and compassion for yourself and others, no matter what's going on inside or out.

The next time you get upset, angry, sad, or whatever, tell yourself it is okay. Just sit with the feeling for a few minutes, alone, and see if it dissipates.

Access the exercises through the membership site at http://tiny.cc/scl-member

Part II - Essential Principles

Now that you have a good background in the fundamentals, the rest of this book lays out twenty-four Soul-Centered Leadership skills designed to be used in your every-day life. By engaging with them, you connect with *yourself*, and start leading from the most powerful place within you: your Authentic Self.

This section draws mainly from psychological techniques that have been tailored towards helping you identify blocks your ego has placed in your consciousness. The exercises with help you find and release those blocks. I've put in a variety of examples from my life and others so you can see how issues show up in everyday experiences, and how you can work with them.

Part III will provide skills based more on spiritual concepts; the "Soul" of Soul-Centered Leadership. They amplify what you learn here.

Keep in mind that this material gains momentum as you progress. Skills and principles build on each other.

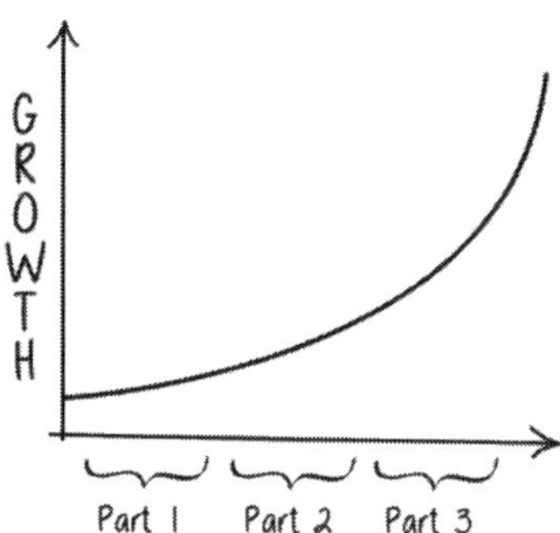

The ARC System

As the Soul-Centered Leadership system contains a lot of skills, I've developed an easy framework system for you that will help you integrate them into your life.

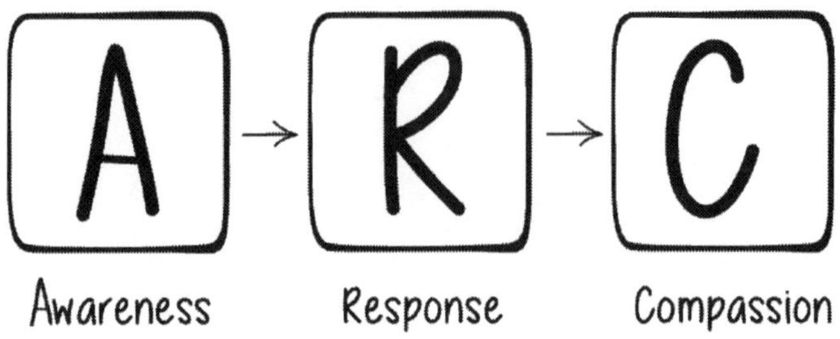

It's called the "ARC System," named for its three components: Awareness, Response, and Compassion.

It's the Swiss-army knife of a Soul-Centered Leader because it can be used anywhere.

Awareness simply means having a true awareness of what's going on. It begins with focusing on yourself. What are you seeing and feeling? How are you reacting? In order to do this, remember what you learned in the mindfulness chapter: no one's ever gained more awareness by speeding up.

When it's time to tap into awareness, stillness and quiet are key. You might be able to achieve this simply by closing your eyes and taking a few deep breaths. For my own part, I put my fingers on the middle of my chest and breathe slowly. This helps me tap into what's going on inside myself.

Response is, of course, the response you choose, as you learned about earlier. We can only control ourselves. That's what this is about. Not instinctual, immediate reaction, but a considered response.

How do you want to respond? What's the highest-level action you can take right now? How can you live your potential?

Compassion is about self-compassion. You are human. You will make mistakes. As you read about the principles and skills and begin applying them, whether they are new to you or not, what you *don't* want to do is to start beating yourself up for all the times in your life you haven't used them—or when you forget to use them even after learning them. That negative self-talk does you no good; in fact, it's counterproductive. So give yourself a break. Remember how we're working on your relationship with yourself? That's what you are strengthening here with the self-compassion.

The ARC system is really that simple. When something's going on, have an awareness of what the real issue is, choose an elevated response, and then go into compassion for you and everyone involved.

In Part IV you'll learn a more powerful ARC system that will allow you to work at a deeper level, one that encompasses all the principles and life integration skills covered in the first three parts. In the meantime, when you learn these principles the ARC system will be reinforced so you will start thinking along the lines of awareness, response and compassion.

Awareness and response will come easily starting right away, and as you get into part three, the self-compassion aspect will be explored in depth.

1. Taking Ownership

Stepping into full ownership is the strongest step a leader can take.

You may be thinking that you already do take responsibility and ownership of things. And I'm sure you are – in certain areas of your life. But do you take it to the level that Soul-Centered Leaders do?

> ***Taking ownership is an extension of control – it's fully focusing on what you can control in order to be the most powerful leader you can be.***

There's a level of ownership that is pervasive and magnificent, one that transcends ego. It takes courage and awareness to engage with such a complete level of ownership, but the results of doing so are transformational. Let me give an example of what I mean.

I knew a business coach who was working with the CEO of a mid-sized firm. The CEO was butting heads with his main salesperson, a lady who had been with him for a long time. Their relationship had been getting worse and worse, and was at the point where they ended up yelling at each other at the end of almost every argument. This happened a few times a week.

You can imagine what effect this had around the office.

The CEO told the coach he wanted to fire the saleslady, but it turned out this would be a potentially disastrous move for the company. She was responsible for 60 percent of new product sales. If he let her go, there would have to be major changes in the company: layoffs, cutting other products, and so on. In fact, it was not even certain the firm would survive.

After suggesting a few strategies that didn't go anywhere, the coach had one more trick up his sleeve. He told the CEO to take her to lunch and apologize. You can imagine how this was received; the CEO reacted by launching into why the saleswoman was wrong, how everything was her fault, and so on and on.

The coach responded by pulling out the roster of employees and asked the CEO which half were going to get laid off after he fires the saleswoman.

This got through to the CEO, and with some coaching, he ultimately followed the advice. He took his employee to lunch, and apologized.

This was no prefab, forced apology. He had done some soul-searching and was sincere. He told her that she was actually doing a great job, that he was acting childish, and that as the leader of the company, he wasn't showing up the way he should be. He took full responsibility, apologized, and asked how he could be a better boss and support her.

The CEO reported back that there was just this silence that seemed to last forever. Just as he was going to ask her if she heard him, the saleswoman started crying. All she ever had ever wanted was to be recognized. Then *she apologized to him* for her part in their rift. They ended up having a fantastic lunch. It turned out that she had a ton of great ideas, and she had never mentioned them because he wouldn't have listened to her.

Now, she's VP of Sales, and she has helped them reach another level.

That CEO took ownership. Let's look at how he did this in terms of the ARC system.

He was *aware* that something needed to change. He was the leader. He couldn't control his employee; he could only control how he shows up. So he owned the situation and looked at ways of changing it. He went from reacting to choosing his *response*. And of course, he didn't waste time dwelling on how he had almost fired her and set his company back years; he had compassion for himself. By putting his ego in his pocket, he stepped up.

Steve Chandler, one of my coaches, calls this moving from victim to ownership.

You can see if you are showing up as a victim or owner by the language (self-talk or talking to others) that you are using.

You want to train yourself to be aware of those moments when you slip into victim thinking. Then change your response to one of ownership. How do you do this?

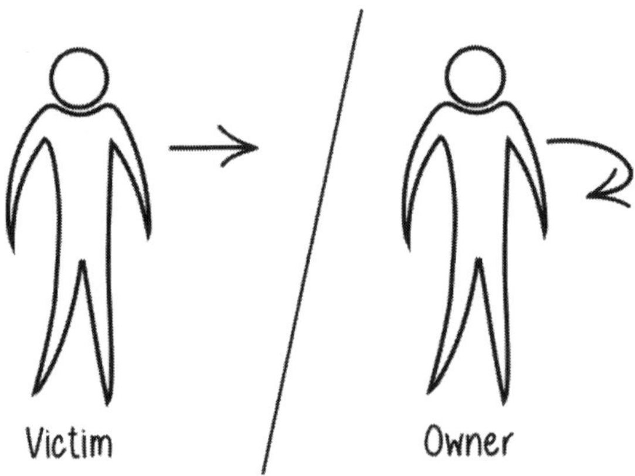

Victimhood versus Ownership

Victimhood is coming from a place of fear, ego. A victim is negative and nitpicky. They tend to feel entitled, helpless, and defensive. They may often be late, and they will typically blame circumstances or other people for the challenges they're facing or the situations in which they find themselves.

Ownership is coming from a place of love. Owners show up positive. They think strategically. They recognize their own role in the situations in which they find themselves, and they hold themselves accountable for how they deal with the challenges (and successes) in their lives. They are proactive, helpful, on time and supportive of others.

You can get a clue of the mindset you or others are in at any given moment by paying attention to the words being used. Victims tend to use words and phrases like *they, but, should, can't, I don't know*. In using these words they reflect a mindset of blame or a reluctance to accept responsibility. If you ask someone in a victim mindset to do something, they're likely to respond with an "I can't," or "I don't know how."

Owners, on the other hand, use words and phrases like *we, I will, I can, I'll find out*. In other words, they focus on themselves and their group in an action-oriented sense. This is the opposite of feeling helpless. The owner asks, "What can I do in this situation? I'm here to solve it. I'll figure it out."

As an entrepreneur, if I stopped anytime I didn't know how to do something, I would have never gotten anywhere. At the very least, Google and YouTube are only a click away! But more to the point, owners know that if they *don't* know something, they can *still* move forward by engaging with the challenge. Victims are more likely to give in to their feelings of doubt when faced with an intimidating problem.

Victims have their happiness and joy dependent on something that normally isn't present:

I'll be happy when...

I'll be happy if...

As in,

"I'll be happy when I get a girlfriend / boyfriend."

"I'll be happy when I get married."

"I'll be happy when I have kids."

"I'll be happy when I get divorced."

"I'll be happy when the kids to go college."

It never ends.

Owners, on the other hand, create their own happiness and joy. They do not make their happiness contingent on getting something, or having a different set of circumstances in their lives.

Owners create their own happiness and joy. They realize there is beauty in each and every moment.

Another contrast: Victims say they didn't have time to get something done.

I didn't have time
?
I didn't make time

"I didn't have time" is not a true statement. "I didn't make time" is the truth. When someone comes to a meeting five minutes late with an excuse like "I couldn't find a parking space" or "My last meeting ran late," they're playing the victim.

The fact is, all of us run late at times. A simple, "I'm sorry I'm late; my bad" will do the trick to let people know you respect their time and that you're accepting responsibility for being late.

Ownership and victimhood are really mindsets, and no one is an "owner" or a "victim" in every aspect of their life all the time. The question you need to ask yourself is, "What's my awareness? Where am I playing the victim in my life, and how can I shift to taking charge as an owner?"

So you can look at your life. How is your career progressing? How much money are you making? How healthy are you? How are your relationships? Are you blaming your failures on others, or on circumstances? If so, you can take ownership right now and change it.

A great question to ask yourself, anytime, is "What am I choosing?" And if you don't like what you hear, change your choice. Change your response.

Embracing ownership in this way can be life changing. In fact, it's the very definition of power.

How do these ideas show up in your leadership?

It's your job as a leader to respond in ownership. Remember, a response is your choice. Your choice should be one of ownership. If you don't own what's happening, no one else will. Think of the leaders you look up to. Do they choose ownership? Or do they whine and complain?

Don't get me wrong: leaders can play the victim. But when they do, they are far less effective, and people tend to follow them more out of fear than respect.

When people come to you with problems and new challenges, what's your first reaction? Then what's your response? Do you go into blaming—or solutions—mode?

Culture of Ownership

This is the single strongest principle I teach to organizations because it's the most immediately effective one. When you can create a "culture of ownership," you and the people around you rise to a whole new level. They quit passing the responsibility and start taking care of things themselves.

Think of your superstar employees. I can guarantee they show up as owners. You have to lead by example to maintain their respect and to show everyone else how it's done. There's no such thing as a leader who plays the victim and has the admiration of their team.

I once did a yearly strategic planning session with a company. We were reviewing their company values, one of which was "tight." I asked what that meant. The CEO responded that they should run a tight ship: Everyone should be on time, prepared, disciplined, and so on.

I asked, "Are you tight? Do you run a tight ship yourself?"

"Yes," he said, without hesitation.

"And yet," I said, gently but directly, "you were late to our last conference call, and you missed the previous one all-together."

He gave me a little laugh then admitted, "Okay, I'm not tight. But I'm the boss. Everyone else has got to be tight."

You can imagine what we spent much of our time talking about after that.

As a leader, you can't ask someone else to take ownership if you're not willing to do so yourself. You can't lie and ask others to be honest. You can't be late and expect others to be on time. Well, technically you can, but in doing so you undermine your own leadership. It's a misalignment. Not only will others see this in you and respond negatively; you will see it in yourself, and it will eventually undercut your self-esteem.

As we go through this book, you will see that authenticity, integrity, and alignment are key to establishing yourself as a Soul-Centered Leader. And these qualities go hand in hand with assuming ownership.

It takes discipline and intention to consistently show up in ownership. It takes a change in mindset. The reward is loyalty and respect.

Ownership is appreciated by those around you. It earns you loyalty and respect; the kind that you don't have to ask for—that's given to you. And it lasts.

Earn your Reputation

I was very active in the San Diego chapter of Entrepreneurs Organization (EO), the largest global organization of entrepreneurial business owners in the world, and I put effort into showing up as an owner. I was on-time, prepared, and engaged in everything.

One of the members there asked me to come in and work with his managers, executives, and high-potential employees. My first meeting I laid out my expectations for everyone: We will always start on time, make and fulfill commitments, and be fully engaged. The owner, who was there with us, said "Yes, I figured. That's what you're known for. That's why you're here."

To me, that was the best compliment I could get. I was showing up as an owner, people took notice, and they wanted some of what I was living.

When you consistently show up as an owner, everyone else does too. You don't have to teach them, they'll just start. Or they'll find their own way out.

In Real Life

Here are some common words / phrases that can identify the mindset of an individual.

Victim	Owner
Negative	Positive
Blaming	Solutions/Supportive
Entitled	Accountable
Defensive	Proactive
Helpless	Helpful
Late	Early
"They"	"We/I"
"I should..."	"I will..."
"But..."	"And..."
"It's not fair"	"It doesn't matter"
"I can't..."	"I can..."
"I don't know"	"I'll find out"

Scan your own awareness and mindset. In what areas of your life do you feel entitled? Where are you defensive? Making excuses? Is something not fair? It is someone else's fault? Are you a victim?

After you do this, it's time to shift gears. Challenge yourself to take ownership in both small and large situations. How many times do you not speak up or take an extra step? Start doing that—a little at a time at first is fine—and see how even the smallest things change.

Go to the Exercises for this chapter (on the Membership Site) to walk through a guided process to come into more personal responsibility and ownership in your life.

Access the exercises through the membership site at http://tiny.cc/scl-member

2. Developing Ownership

Who in your life comes to you with their problems?

Maybe it's your sales director who complains the market's in a rut. Or your operations manager who says she can't find qualified people. Or your friend who always has so much drama around them and calls you to cry on your shoulder.

Should I even bring up family members?

Your first desire is probably to be compassionate and comfort them. Your response may be something like "Yeah, I know it's tough. I'm really sorry to hear that. Just keep at it. I know things will turn around for you."

What are you really doing talking with them this way?

You're actually keeping them in the victim mindset. This can be called co-dependence or enabling. You are reinforcing the idea that their behavior is fine. You might as well be saying, "Go ahead, stay there. I'll commiserate with you. Life is hard and that's just the way it is."

This may sound too hardcore, but if we look at this practically, are you really helping them this way? After a few minutes of compassion, can any good come out of it? Your response is actually ego-based, as you have fear that if you tell them the truth, you may be rejected by them. Or maybe you don't like confrontation and conflict, so it's uncomfortable as you secretly think about how long you will be stuck there with them.

Soul-Centered Leaders take others from victim to ownership. It's not always an easy or fun conversation. But it's the single biggest gift you can give them. And as a Soul-Centered Leader, it's your duty.

A more elevated response might sound something like this: "Yes, I know that's a problem. The question is what are you going to do about it? I'm here to help you brainstorm and support. Come on, we can do this together." That message comes from a place of love, and when you deliver it with care and empowerment; you're not making anyone wrong. Rather, you are supporting them with moving forward.

And if they persist on telling you what's wrong, mirror back to them what you are hearing. "You know, you're really focused on what's not working. I'm here to help you make things work regardless. What I can do is help you figure out ways to overcome your challenges. Though right now you are stuck in complaining. Let me know when you're ready to move forward."

Harsh? Maybe. Effective? You bet[1].

It's Their Choice

Not long ago I had lunch with someone who was being negative. She spent our first twenty minutes together telling me what was wrong with everything in her life. I reflected back my awareness of her negativity and offered some suggestions to her on ways she could change her response.

She wasn't interested. She said there was nothing she could do.

I told her gently but firmly that I thought she was mistaken. I made it clear that I teach people how to change this thinking, and I've seen that when people choose on their own to take ownership, it changes everything.

She didn't want to hear it. We won't be having lunch again.

Personally, I don't care where people are on their evolutionary ladder. I only care if they have the intention to keep on evolving and elevating.

If people don't even have the intention to move from victimhood to ownership, they're not going to move no matter what

[1] I realize, of course, that different situations call for different measures. If, for example, someone has just been through a traumatic event and is feeling raw pain or shock, they may not at all be playing the victim and may need a different kind of support.

you do. Then you have to decide if you really want that person in your company or life.

There's more on this in the chapter about effective communication in the Boundaries section.

Group Victimhood and Ownership

You have to be very careful to pay attention to where and when victimhood pops up. It can appear at the individual, group, departmental, and even organizational level. For example, if the general tone in your sales department is "Nothing's working; we aren't getting any leads," that's a victimhood mentality. It may or may not be true—that this is a challenging time for the department—but the point is that you can either hide behind ambiguous excuses or find ways to make the necessary changes when something's not working.

It's happened to me too, of course. The company I owned and ran was a software reseller for a major technology company. I constantly complained about a perceived lack of support from this company, the slow development of its products, and issues with its partner programs. Others in my organization took my lead and started complaining about the tech company as well. It became pervasive throughout my own company, until my business coach brought it to my awareness.

So the next quarterly meeting I took full ownership for it.

I owned that it was up to me to change my behavior, my response (or reaction) and my attitude. As a group we decided to hold each other accountable for this adjustment. All of a sudden it seemed like there were less issues with the software company. Relationships with their reps improved. Leads increased. Work became easier and more fun.

Taking Too Much Ownership

The concept of ownership can play out in unexpected ways, including ones that at first might seem counterintuitive. For example, there may be places where you are taking too much ownership. Consider where you might be engaging in "over-responsibility."

Are there areas in your organization where you find yourself covering for people who aren't fulfilling their responsibilities? Maybe somebody turns something in that's 80 percent complete but still needs some finessing to make it work with the project at hand—so instead of handing it back to them you just do it yourself? Or perhaps someone is distracted and you feel like it's easier to just do a job yourself rather than holding them accountable and handing it off?

Over-responsibility is another ego-based reaction. There may be a couple things at work here. Your ego may want to be needed, to help you "prove" your "value." Maybe part of you wants to simply show off a bit: "Look how smart and talented I am!" Another part might be trying to position you above others: "I'm the only one who gets anything done around here." Still another angle might be that you're simply impatient and not giving someone enough time to do their job.

In a sense, all of these reactions spring from victimhood masquerading as ownership.

It takes a deft touch for a leader to know when to let your people deal with a tough situation by themselves in order to truly take in the learning. As leaders, we often are good at fixing things. However, when we fix everything, people don't learn and grow. This habit shows up in our personal lives too, especially with entrepreneurs. We show our love and affection for people by "fixing" their lives.

Is this you? When your spouse, kids, or friends come to you, do you automatically go into fix-it mode? If you do, you're actually creating a barrier between yourself and them; you're placing yourself above them in a manner of speaking. As in, "I know better than you; here let me show you what you should do." If you and the other person get too comfortable in those roles, they'll keep relying on you and it becomes an unequal, codependent relationship.

This is why a lot of business owners lack intimacy in their personal relationships. Healthy relationships are not based on fixing someone's problems.

When it comes to your family and friends, just focus on being present and with them. You don't need to fix anything. Just be there. Believe it or not, as a Soul-Centered Leader, often just your positive, strong presence will be something that inspires people and gives them strength. In this sense, ownership is about understanding that there are natural processes for both individuals and in life itself. Sometimes the best way to "own" a situation is recognizing what your proper role is in it—and sticking to it rather than overstepping your boundaries.

In Real Life

When people come to you with an issue, see if you can coach them into taking full ownership of it. Resist the urge to "fix" it or simply hand them the solution. Guide them with questions like:

- Well, that's out of your control; what can you control?
- What are you going to do to resolve the issue?
- I hear what you don't like about it. What do you like? What could the benefits be?
- Do you consider this to be your responsibly to fix? Why not?

See the exercises in this chapter to work a process of moving others into ownership.

Access the exercises through the membership site at http://tiny.cc/scl-member.

3. Commitments

Many people get what they want to do and what they commit to doing mixed up. I'm sure there is a lot of things you want to do, don't get those confused with what you commit to doing.

A commitment is something you absolutely, positively will make happen.

A commitment is a decision that you are 100% in. That means if you are bringing 99% or less to the table and you aren't absolutely sure you will do something, don't commit to it.

How often do these come up?

- You promise to send something to someone by Tuesday, and you send it first thing Wednesday morning.
- You arrive at a meeting a few minutes late; even meetings that you schedule and are leading.
- You bump into an old friend and say "we should get together" or "I'll give you a call," but part of you knows that you won't reach out after this short encounter.
- You let an employee know that you will meet with them for their review on a certain date; then you miss that meeting at the last minute because you get busy with something.
- You have a conference call at 9:00 AM, and to you it means you start dialing the phone at 9:00. This means you join a few minutes late, and people are either waiting for you or already talking.

Each of these is a broken commitment. They are cases of you not being in integrity and losing a little – or a lot – of respect from others.

It's poor leadership. Plain and simple.

If you've let seemingly small commitments slip, you probably don't think it's a big deal. Yet what if you are the person on the other side of the equation? If someone promises something on a certain day but delivers it to you the next, do you notice? I sure do. Every time someone is late to a meeting or conference call, even if I don't bring it up, I make a mental note: Hmmmm . . . This person might not be so reliable. Be careful what I trust them with. Don't you have that little ticker when people don't fulfill what they promise you? I'm not sure if I've ever met anyone who hasn't.

Internal Commitments

What about commitments you make to yourself? These are as important as ones you make to others.

"Ah I have to read that book."

"I'm not going to drink tonight."

"I'm going to start exercising next week."

"I'm never ever going to make that mistake again."

We've all made claims like this to ourselves, and we've all let at least some of them fall away without acting on them. How often do you personally make a promise to yourself that you don't fulfill? Remember, this is not about getting down on you. It is about coming into a place of greater integrity.

> ***Every time you break a commitment to yourself, you are moving in a direction that is opposite the direction that you want to move in.***

The rules for making commitments to yourself are the same as they are for those you make to others. In both cases, be very clear about what you are committing to. Commitments are specific and time-bound. At the end of the day, you've either completed it or you haven't.

When someone tells me they'll have something to me by Tuesday, I ask them what they mean by that. Noon? Midnight? When? Because when it's not specific, I may be expecting it during the day, when you may be planning on sending it just before midnight. This is crucial for everyone, including the person making the commitment. When the deadline is clear there's no need to play the game of shifting the goalposts. It brings a layer of efficiency and clarity to your work.

What I want you to focus on from here on out is actually making fewer commitments. Especially the small ones, where you are setting yourself up for failure, or where a commitment isn't necessary. So, for example:

- When you see an old friend on the street, instead of saying, "We should get together" or, "I'll call you soon"—which you know you aren't going to do—say instead, "Nice to see you."
- How many books do you hear about and tell yourself, I have to read that one too! Do you ever start thinking, Wow, I have all these books on my reading list. I'm overwhelmed just thinking about it. So instead, from now on when you see a good book, change your inner talk to say like That sounds interesting. If I have the time and space, maybe I'll read it. This may seem like a small shift, but it supports you by putting things in the right perspective. You can't read all the great books out there, so you shouldn't commit yourself to the task, only to feel badly about it later.
- Instead of telling someone that you'll have a deliverable to them by Tuesday, assess your schedule and maybe give yourself until Thursday. Then deliver early. If they need it earlier, it's up to them to let you know that.

Looking at commitments this way often leads to a simpler life, one where you take on less and, as a result, generate less stress and anxiety. Knowing what to expect of yourself allows you to get things done much more effectively, accurately and successfully.

Renegotiating Commitments

In the rare cases that you can't fulfill a commitment—which happens even with best of intentions—renegotiate the commitment.

Renegotiating a commitment means that as soon as you know you won't be able to fulfill it, you let anyone who is involved in the process know.

If you have a 9:30 AM meeting and there's a wreck on the freeway that's backed up traffic for an hour, call the other attendees as soon as you know and move the meeting back. Don't just show up late and make an excuse. It's only a renegotiation if you initiate it before the commitment is due—as soon as you know and with a suggestion for a new agreement. It's taking ownership for your actions, or lack of actions, and respecting others.

If you are supposed to send a report or proposal to someone and you become fairly sure that you can't deliver it by the promised date, have a conversation with the other party. Take the pressure off of yourself and let them know where you're at and why. See if it's really an issue with them. Set new expectations. Then you are back in integrity, you still have their trust, and you can work on the project without this dark cloud over you.

Of course, this will work if you are not simply making excuses, and particularly if you have proven yourself in other ways. If you find yourself frequently renegotiating commitments, you need to revisit the process whereby you make them in the first place.

All of this applies to renegotiating your internal commitments as well. If you commit to working out three days a week and break your arm, tell yourself that you will start working out one week after the doctor says it's okay to do.

The result of becoming stronger in your commitments is that you start to trust yourself again. You become mindful of your energy (all of which we will discuss later). And other people will trust you more too. You become a person of integrity.

Positioning Yourself for Success

Often people are in the habit of making things difficult – if not impossible – on themselves. Part of creating better integrity around commitments involves making sure that when you commit to something, it's specific and doable within a specific timeframe. Confirm these points in writing so that there's no grey area; for example, send an e-mail to all relevant parties with the details. Explain to them what a renegotiation is. You don't do this to micromanage or "keep them on their toes" in a negative way; rather you do it to remove the elements of ambiguity that can interfere with the smooth completion of the project. No one has to stop to wonder, "What did we say about that?" You always have that written commitment to refer back to.

Let me show you how a normal conversation goes after telling someone about commitments.

I ask a client, "Okay, since you haven't been exercising, do you want to make a commitment around that?"

They reply, "Yes! I used to be a runner, so how about I run for an hour every day next week?"

"Hmmm . . . Is that something you can commit to? You told me you haven't run for a few years. An hour a day seems pretty intense."

"You're right. How about thirty minutes?"

"Why not just commit to ten minutes? Then if you run thirty you'll be ahead of the game."

"Okay, I'll do that, every day next week."

"What does next week look like for you?"

"Well, I have to go to Atlanta for three days for a big conference."

"Will you be able to run when you are in Atlanta?"

"Probably not."

"Okay, then you probably don't want to commit to running every day, do you?"

You can see how people need to be coached on their commitments, to think through want they can commit to and what they can't. The same holds true for our own personal commitments. In fact, you could argue that this might even be truer, because at the speed of thought we can make all sorts of commitments in our heads that we could never hope to complete. This is why writing things down is just as important when we make personal commitments.

Can you imagine the productivity in your organization and your personal life when everything that is said and agreed to gets done? Think, too, of the trust that will grow between team members, and the loyalty that will be earned with your clients.

Let me tell you, when you and your whole team are nailing your commitments, it's a beautiful thing.

In Real Life

Start having a process you run through before you commit to something. Does it deserve to be a commitment? Are you specific about it? Is the timeframe realistic? Fast-forward in your mind, thinking of everything on your to-do list, and determine if you have the time and the energy to commit, and if it is something you really want to take on.

When people ask us to do things—for example, be on a board or a committee—we often want to say "yes" right away. We want to help out whoever is asking, or we have fear it's a one-time offer and we will miss out if we don't say "yes" (This is also referred to as FOMO—Fear Of Missing Out!). Make a new rule for yourself; anytime you get a request such as this, let the person asking know that you'll let them know the next day. This gives you time to think about it and really assess if it's the right thing for you at this time.

I once heard someone say that a CEO will only be as successful as their ability to say "no," because a talent for saying "no" as needed keeps them focused on the important things. I see so many people over committing to things in their life. To effect real change, you need to become an expert, a master of something, and that requires focus. Quit putting tons of different things on your plate and excel at one thing. At the end of the day, that's often more fun anyway!

Go through the exercises to get more authentic and conscious about your commitments.

Access the exercises through the membership site at http://tiny.cc/scl-member.

4. From Judgments to Acceptance

When something happens, there's only one truth about it. That "it is". That it happened. (I know, I'm talking abstract, just bear with me...)

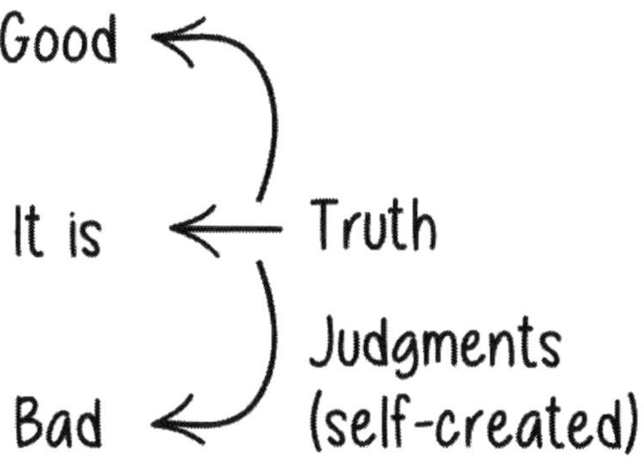

When something happens, we as humans often complicate things by assigning a "good" or "bad" to it—a positive or negative charge. That assignment, that charge, is the judgment. We often do this in flash, without deeply thinking or contemplating what happened. In short, we react. This is a very normal, human thing to do.

Say my girlfriend breaks up with me. I think, "What's wrong with me? I'm a loser! I'll always be alone!" That's a negative judgment. It's me choosing to assign a negative to it.

Or I could think, "That's great - she wasn't the right woman for me, and I guess I wasn't the right guy for her. Glad we both found that out now instead of later."

Both are judgments, one negative, one positive.

But strip away these judgments for a moment and you can see there's really only one truth in the matter: my girlfriend broke up with me. That "it is"...it happened.

The same is true regardless of the situation. Sales are down. Sales are up. I missed my flight. My kid aced her math test but got a C in history. I got a new job. I got laid off.

Each of these events simply is. They exist pre-judgment.

Is it good or bad that I missed my flight? Neither: it is.

Is it good or bad that sales are down? Neither: it is.

Acceptance is recognizing and coming into peace with this. Whereas judgment is often (though not always) negative, acceptance comes from a place of love—from the Authentic Self.

I accept this person whether or not I agree with everything they do. It's not my place to say how they live their life. It's just up to me how I choose to respond.

I accept that my girlfriend broke up with me. That's simply what's happening at the moment.

A Key Life and Leadership Skill

Moving out of judgment and into acceptance can be life-changing.

For one thing, automatic judgments tend to trigger automatic reactions. Consider how this affects your decision making. When you judge something you bring emotion into the mix. When you make decisions, are they best made from an emotional state or a rational, neutral state?

I don't know about you, but when I look back on all my poor decisions, they sure weren't made from an accepting point of view. I was embroiled in emotion. But when we move into a state of acceptance, everything is just information. We see more clearly, without clouding judgments, and this allows us to make decisions with a clear head, taking everything into account properly.

Another thing is that a negative judgment is ego-driven. It comes from a place of fear. Thoughts fill our head, things like: This is a terrible thing! I won't have enough money. I'm all alone and I'll always be. I'm better than this person. Everyone's better than me. Everything's out of control.

Keep in mind that negative judgments are self-created. In fact, you're more in control of them than you think. When you feel that something "bad" has happened, know that you, at some level, assigned the negative charge to the situation. Knowing this allows you to see that you can un-assign the negativity just as quickly as you assigned it. We'll look at how to do this soon, but let me mention one more reason why shifting from judgment to acceptances can be so powerful: It takes so much energy to move up and down the scale of judgments.

When I was running two of my software companies, I would judge everything. I would have a call with a potential prospect that went well, and I would get sky-high. A minute later, an employee would come in and say they were taking a few days off; I would think it was the end of the world. My day was a roller coaster of emotions, up and down, and by the end of it I was exhausted.

But when I took to heart what I learned about judgments and acceptance, the difference in my experience was amazing. As things happened at work, I would remind myself that all I was getting was information. Things aren't good or bad, they just are. And I took it as my job as the leader to come to the table calm and level-headed.

The difference was like night and day. My stress level reduced by half. My energy level stayed high the whole day through. I was making much better decisions, especially in times of crisis. And people around me noticed the difference too. They remarked about how calming a presence I had become. I earned their trust as a leader because I was calm under pressure and would show the way forward in sticky situations.

All this led me to become more of a Soul-Centered Leader. Because the Soul, the Self, has no judgments. It loves and accepts absolutely everything.

When you react with negativity it pushes people away. They start to work in fear of making you angry. After a time, people will try to hide things from you. Even if you don't mean to intimidate or bully, you're still the leader, and people don't want to upset the boss. Often you end up developing a team of "yes" men and women, just telling you what you want to hear. This works well for a while, until everything comes tumbling down because people have been avoiding important issues for fear of upsetting you.

Acceptance, like everything else, can be a learned skill. It just takes intention, time and focus.

As you start to adopt acceptance as a practice, you will see your leadership abilities skyrocket. Your energy level, decision making, and stress management will improve dramatically.

A great leader doesn't stomp their feet or shoot the messenger when something happens—they buckle down and solve the problem.

Keep in mind that you're never going to eliminate all judgments. They're part of the human experience, but with just a little bit of work, you can greatly minimize them—and the negative impact they can have. And when you go into judgment, you can become aware of it quickly and choose acceptance as a higher-level response.

Evaluations versus Judgments

In the truest sense, there is no good or bad. We could say there are things that serve us, and don't serve us. Or are healthy, or unhealthy. Or that we want to align ourselves with, or do not. To that end, consider the difference between an evaluation and a judgment.

Making an evaluation is different from making a judgment. An evaluation is making a decision about something without the positive or negative charge. It's absolutely healthy to make evaluations, which can be done without ever making the other person wrong.

Say there is someone you do business with who you've found has been dishonest.

Here is how you might describe this person with a judgment: "That guy is a freaking liar. I'm never going to trust that idiot!"

Here is how you might sound coming from a place of acceptance: "That guy has been dishonest with me multiple times now. This isn't good for me or for the business. I'm choosing not to do business with him."

See the difference? In the latter case you're accepting the situation and the other person and choosing to not be aligned with whatever unhealthy behavior he's engaged in, or whatever he's doing that doesn't align with how you choose to live your life. It's an informed and strategic decision.

Coming from a place of judging results in a more emotional reaction. Granted, it may have the same end result as acceptance—not working with the individual in question—but it might also lead to burning bridges in a less professional way or some other retaliatory action. At the very least, coming from a place of acceptance allows you to maintain your equilibrium, and it lets you be the kind of positive, empowering leader you want to be.

Accepting versus Agreeing

There's also a difference between agreeing with someone or a situation, and accepting it. You always can be in acceptance, even when you don't agree with something.

Say someone steals my wallet. I could choose to emotionally react: get upset, freak out over losing my credit cards, despair that I'll have to spend hours on the phone sorting it out, and get angry as hell with the dirty thief who took it. Then I could call a friend and get him to commiserate with me about how it sucks that my wallet was stolen, and how I'm such a victim.

Or, instead of getting all worked up, I accept the situation. Now that the wallet's gone, what's the next smartest action I can take? I go ahead and alert the authorities, credit card companies, etc. When the police catch the person, I go ahead and take action and prosecute. After all, I still believe in boundaries and rules.

Which option do you think works better for me? What helps me get on with my life more quickly, without draining my energy and making a bad situation worse?

When I hear on the news about someone getting killed, raped, or any other tragedy, I am conscious of my energy. I do sometimes catch myself saying, "What a bad person, this world sucks," but I move to acceptance and compassion for everyone involved. Again, I am not agreeing with what that person did, but I don't find it helpful to put myself in a negative state of mind. That's not helping anyone.

In fact, sometimes I tell myself to quit playing the victim by wallowing in my negativity, and instead direct that energy into positive action, into being a part of the solution. I pick up the phone and donate, volunteer, or whatever I can do.

Sometimes people who let social situations weigh on them because they consider them too big to solve (homelessness, healthcare, etc.) often aren't doing anything to help solve the problem. This isn't because their intentions aren't good. It's because the sheer emotional weight of focusing on the challenges our society faces can make one feel helpless. But by getting involved, even on a small, local level, you can see how your action affects the individuals, and that weight gets lifted.

This, too, is a form of acceptance. You accept that the world has significant problems to address, but you can also accept that you can only contribute to helping—the burden is not yours alone.

In Real Life

When you catch yourself in negativity, break it down. What is truth? What is the "it is" in the situation? And how are you choosing to respond?

When a situation arises that you could deem negative, tell yourself, "This is simply information. I'm the leader here. What's the most elevated, uplifting way I can address this situation?" In fact, most likely you've handled things much more intense.

Keep in mind that your job as a leader is to solve issues. When people come to you with something that you might normally have responded to with a negative judgment, take the attitude that "I'm a Soul-Centered Leader. It's my role to show up to this situation strong and be a model for elevated leadership."

When you're around other people who are talking negatively about someone else, just simply say, "Well I don't want to judge them." Almost all the time, the person talking moves out of judgment and focuses on the facts.

Work through the exercises in this chapter to identify your judgments and clear them.

Access the exercises through the membership site at http://tiny.cc/scl-member.

5. Releasing Attachments

Buddhists call attachment the root of all suffering. And I don't know about you, but I've been through enough suffering in my life.

An attachment is an expectation. Being attached to a specific outcome means you have put emotional energy into it. You're waiting for something to happen, and if it doesn't you will judge yourself as a failure or not be happy. It can happen in any area of your life. Maybe you're attached to making a certain amount of money, having a big deal close, achieving some sort of status. You might be attached to the idea of getting married, having kids, having grandkids.

When you let go of attachments, you live free, and you get rid of the suffering you have been causing yourself.

While it's okay to have a preference that something will go your way, when you have an attachment to it, you've invested yourself in a certain outcome. You're saying, "I'll only be happy if..." and then your happiness is tied to an external circumstance. If you don't achieve it, this leads to disappointment and upset. It takes you out of the present moment and clouds your judgment about yourself and others. It's like the ego creates a picture of how something should be and invests energy, even your sense of self, into it. If it isn't achieved, there is a letdown.

Releasing attachments doesn't mean you'll never feel disappointment, or you won't care which way things turn out. As I said above, having a preference about the way things go is perfectly normal, and it allows us to direct our energy into what we want to create. But when we're attached to an outcome it's as if the energy we've invested in it backfires on us if we don't achieve it, and gets channeled into upset and feelings of failure.

Free Yourself by Releasing the Attachment

Here's the funny thing about your higher power and attachments. When you are attached to an outcome, often you will either not achieve it, or when you do, it won't live up to your expectation. For example, I was attached to making a certain amount of money and having a business of a certain size. Once I achieved those, I wasn't happy nor fulfilled. And I just changed my attachment to making more money and having a larger organization.

Once you let go of your attachment and are truly okay living without it, then what you want seems to appear. And it's better than you originally thought it would be.

It's like your higher power is playing with you, teaching you the hard way that resistance is futile and you're never truly in control.

So how do you let go of something as abstract as an attachment? Start by visualizing it.

The response you can choose to let go of an attachment is to simply let it go. Picture yourself holding the attachment, and letting it go.

Let it fly away, and whatever happens, know that you're OK with it. If you were waiting to be happy or fulfilled once your desired outcome appeared, remind yourself that you can be happy and fulfilled right now, by choosing to be.

Simple, isn't it?

Look at all the places you might have attachments in your life. Relationships? Income? Goals?

Imagine you're going to interview someone for a key position and you really think they'll be a good fit, but you're really attached to having them join your firm and fill this open slot. Then they come in and you just don't connect. You get that familiar feeling that they aren't the right person for your organization.

Your attachment could drive one of two outcomes: either you pull the trigger anyway, bringing someone on board whom your intuition tells you isn't a good fit, or after the interview you enter a mood of upset because you were attached to having them join.

Now if you weren't attached to having them fill the slot, you could have saved your energy and simply moved on. Your head would have been clear for strategizing what to do next. See how much pain you can save yourself?

The Results of Attachments

There are areas where whole companies have to be cautious about attachments.

If you've ever had a large prospect that people are banking on, that's an attachment. Salespeople start counting their commissions, managers start spending their additional budget, and the owners are calculating how much extra money they will be bringing in. Celebrations start early.

Then it doesn't happen and spirits are crushed.

The same can be true if your company is the target of, or is targeting, acquisition. It can be easy to put so much stock into whether or not it happens. Then, if the process gets delayed and the negotiations drag on, it can put you at a physical, mental, and emotional disadvantage. Your energy is tied up in what might happen rather than what's going on in the moment. Meantime whatever's happening in the present moment suffers from this diversion of energy.

> ***When you let go of attachments, you are calm under pressure. Others will see this shift in energy and be drawn to you. This automatically puts you in a position of influence, authentic power, and leadership.***

It's your job to manage expectations. Keep everyone in line. Remind them that not everything is in their control and that another direction is always a possibility. This will not only keep people focused on what they can influence—it will put you in a better mindset for negotiation and leadership.

Lead with Clarity and Strength

I was working with a business owner who had tremendous success. He had taken his business from zero to $10 million in about ten years by bootstrapping it and having the business self-fund its own growth. This, in case you don't know, almost never, ever happens.

Then his industry went in the tank and his company leveled off from the growth. It didn't even go into decline; rather, revenue and profits just stayed the same for a six-month period. For many this might be something to pay attention to, but not a crisis—certainly not an indication of failure.

But it had a devastating effect on my client. In his mind, he was no longer this butt-kicking, rebel CEO who was growing by leaps and bounds. He considered himself a failure. He was so attached to the growth—something that he couldn't control, and something unsustainable—that when it subsided he dove deep into depression. All of a sudden he was desperate to sell his firm. A few private equity companies wanting to enter his market saw the state of mind he was in and the company's lack of growth over the recent period and presented him with several lowball offers.

He ended up coming to me before accepting any of them. We worked on getting him to let go of his attachments (and his identities). Systematically, using the exact same exercises that are in this book, we found out where his ego was holding tightly to certain outcomes, and my client learned to let go of them.

The work ended up turning around his life. He moved out of the depression and into the strong, driven leader he had been before the downturn. He decided not to sell the company right then; instead he buckled down, toughed out the hard times, strengthened his business, and re-engaged when he could drive the terms of the deal. By the time he finally decided to sell the company, its growth, profits, and revenue were on the upswing, and he got a significantly better deal.

In this case learning to let go of his attachments brought him, literally, millions of dollars more than he would have made otherwise, as well as much better overall terms on the sale. His didn't let his fear of scarcity win out. He had the strength and confidence to wait until the good times to sell.

In Real Life

What are you attached to happening? What are you counting on coming through?

Common areas in our lives where we get attached to outcomes include:

- Closing a prospect
- Having a problem client or employee improve
- Getting a capital infusion
- Selling all or part of a company
- Filling a position
- Growing a company in a certain way
- Having a relationship with someone (at work or in our private lives)

Keep in mind there are always two options for an outcome: 1) It may happen, or 2) It may not. Which outcome are you attached to and how is this attachment affecting you?

Go to the exercises section of this chapter to list and begin clearing attachments in your life.

Access the exercises through the membership site at http://tiny.cc/scl-member.

6. Authentic Communication

A tight, high-performing team is one that has great communication. While many of the tools in this book teach this, there are a few that deserve a specific section in this chapter. You may know some or all of these already; however I've worked to simply them and give clear direction on how to implement them in yourself and the workplace. They are the keys to more trust, less confusion, stronger company culture, and ultimately better results.

Setting Clear Agreements

Let's start with disappointment. (This is another great Steve Chandler nugget.)

> ***Disappointment is almost always a result of unclear agreements.***

Think of the last time you experienced disappointment with another person. Most likely there was a "sort-of" agreement between you and the other individual. You took one assumption to fill in the blanks, and they took another.

Here's an example. You have an employee who works seven hours a day. You sit down and ask him to work more hours, he agrees. He starts working seven and half hours a day. You expected nine. You get disappointed. You mention that you had expected him to work longer, and he's upset – because he has been working more. Just not the nine hours you were hoping for.

Did you have an agreement? Yes: to work more. Did you specify what "working more" means? No, you didn't. The result? Disappointment.

Yes, there are times when specific agreements are made which don't get fulfilled. That's a different case—and refer back to the chapter on commitments for more on that. Most people, though, are good at getting things done; everyone just has to be clear on what "getting done" means. We do this by creating specific agreements, not by relying on an assumption that we're on the same page with someone else.

It's also important not to bully people into making agreements. For example, I've noticed in my own case that if I'm not mindful, I can use my strong personality to get someone to agree to something. The problem with this is that it isn't a clean agreement. It's ego-based—I'm asserting myself from a place of ego, and they're responding from one as well—and often people will not complete that agreement because of conscious or subconscious resentment. This, of course, can only lead to more disappointment.

So when laying out what you would like to agree on with someone, it's important that your share a solid understanding of the terms of the agreement, and that both parties choose to enter into it together. No one should feel pressure around it.

Setting Clear Boundaries

Boundaries are often overlooked, not clarified, not communicated, and not adhered to. This leads to breakdowns in communication, relationships, and trust. How good are you at expressing them, both with others as well as yourself?

A boundary is a clear line that you draw signifying exactly what you will allow and not allow.

Examples of boundaries are;

- You can call me in the evening, but not after 8 PM.
- I cannot guarantee that I will answer an e-mail the same day; if you need me urgently, send me a text message.
- If you are going to miss a delivery date, I need to know by noon at least one business day beforehand, so I can support you.
- There are times you yell at me; it's best if you only talk to me when you are calm so I can understand you. Can we agree on

that?

It's important that you deliver your boundaries wrapped in care and compassion. When doing so, focus on what your own experience is and make plain that your boundary is not passively making the person you're talking to wrong. I call this kind of delivery neutral honesty as you are talking about yourself, which is all you truly know about, and not projecting onto the other person, which will make them defensive.

Finally, make sure you state it in positive terms.

For example, do you have someone in your life that is negative? Someone who frequently complains or criticizes others? How would you set a boundary with them?

It might look like this: "Hey, Joe, we work together a lot, and we usually seem to have a good thing going. I'd like to keep our conversations focused on the positive things that happen. I've noticed that sometimes they drift into gossip and criticism, which I certainly know I've initiated at times. I'm working to have less of that in my life. Can you support me in this? Can we agree on no more negativity in our conversations, and to focus on the positive?"

How would anyone say no to that? Notice, too, that I didn't say anything about Joe being negative. In the above example, once the agreement is set, if one of us goes into the negative, either of us can bring them back to this agreement.

> ***Boundaries clear up ambiguity in the relationship, and they allow for more trust and support.***

Clarity in Communication

Overall, people want to do a good job. It's up to you as a leader to give them the structure, tools, and information to do it. And as always, that starts with you. By cleaning up and strengthening your communication, you will gain that inherent influence that Soul-Centered Leaders have.

So you have to start becoming crystal clear in your communications. What are your boundaries? What are your commitments?

What are your expectations and agreements? Exactly what are they? This leads to trust on both ends, and thus to high-performance.

At this point you might be thinking, "This is helpful information, but what about the spiritual aspect? I thought this was 'Soul-Centered Leadership.'" It's true: a lot of what we're covering here is emotional intelligence with some psychology thrown in (more of which will be coming up later in Part II). What I've found is that you have to be rock-solid on the physical, mental, emotional, and unconscious levels before going into the spiritual levels. They're like building blocks, and as you get comfortable with them you can go higher and higher, closer, in a manner of speaking, to your higher power. That's why we call it "elevating the consciousness." These tools are the foundation, and they will allow you to strengthen your relationship with yourself, others, and your higher power.

So hang in there and enjoy the ride!

In Real Life

When you experience disappointment with another person, look back; was there an agreement made that wasn't specific? Go back and talk through it with the other person. Look for misalignments between your understandings of the situation that you're dealing with.

Clean up your agreements! The next time you get buy-in from someone, lay out a very specific agreement. Ask for feedback from the other party and make sure they know they can say "no"—otherwise their "yes" won't be authentic and they won't be fully bought in.

What boundaries do you need to set to free up more space and energy in your life? Where are there areas of discontent in your life, and how can setting a boundary help you take control of them?

Go to the exercises in this chapter to deepen your agreements and boundaries.

Access the exercises through the membership site at http://tiny.cc/scl-member

7. Identities

The ego is a crafty bugger, and it has many ways to hide its behavior from you. When it comes to identities—how you perceive yourself—for example, it tricks you into thinking that its own ego-based behavior is simply a normal part of your makeup.

How many times have you excused or rationalized something you did because you called yourself a boss, woman, man, husband, wife, son, daughter, brother, sister, grandparent, grandchild, customer, owner, entrepreneur, friend, adult, kid, Dodger fan, Patriots fan, American, Jew, Christian, Muslim, Buddhist, and on and on and on?

Here are some examples:

- You act rudely to your personal assistant, because you're a harried executive.
- You work 80 hours a week, because that's what owners "have to" do.
- You're loud and don't follow rules, because you're an entrepreneur; those rules aren't meant for you!
- You never show any vulnerability to your team, because that's not something bosses do.
- You yell at your kids and justify it by saying, "I'm allowed to do that! I'm your parent!"
- You always keep your mate waiting, because that's what women do.
- You don't show any emotion, because that's just what men do.

See what's happening here? Your ego creates this view of yourself based on an "identity," and you end up using it as an excuse to hide behind. If you're acting a certain way because that's just "who you are," then how can anyone hold you accountable for your behavior or expect you to change? For that matter, how can you ask yourself to change when you're just being "you"?

Identities are a way to play the victim through entitlement; they can help us shirk personal responsibility for change by blaming our actions on our "identity" rather than our own choices.

The fact is that you are none of these identities. You may happen to be a boss, a man, a woman, and so on. Those are roles you may fill. But they're not you.

You are you.

Free Yourself

When I sold my largest company, I moved out of my office and took all of my plaques down; there were around fifteen of them. I had won Social Entrepreneur of the Year, was nominated for Most Admired CEO, was on the Inc. 500 | 5000 Fastest Growing Companies, and more. My realtor came over to discuss some business, saw them piled up, and casually mentioned that she knew someone that had thrown all of their awards and honors away because they only represented material accomplishments.

I thought about this for several days. A lot. At the time I was thinking about a new office where I could post the awards, along with my degrees, on the wall. Why would I do that? It would give me validation as an intelligent, accomplished person. It would make me look so important, so worthy of respect.

But this struck me as such ego-based thinking. (Funnily enough, I've heard the term "ego-wall" to describe the display of one's awards for all to see. Very appropriate.) And since I had this awareness, I chose a different response. My intention was for people to get to know me, not to base our relationship on what I had, or had not, accomplished. To have us connect person-to-person. Not title-to-title or accomplishment-to-accomplishment.

All those things were in the past. They had nothing, really, to do with the present moment. In fact, they took me out of the present moment and moved me into a past-based, ego mindset.

So I threw them all away. Right in the garbage.

I've still accomplished all of those things; throwing the physical representation of them away doesn't erase that. But they are not me. Just as I have done drugs, had a divorce, and been in lawsuits. These aren't me either. They're just things that happened.

You, too, have done many things. Things you're proud of, and things you would rather forget. They are not you. None of them. Don't let them define you. When you start thinking of yourself as simply you so many obligations fall away. You start taking ownership of your decisions and stop hiding behind the identity.

In Real Life

When you meet someone, how soon is it until you bring up your title, what you do, how much money you earn, how big your company / team is, what you own, where you live, what school you went to, what family you came from, or anything like that? Check in with yourself. Where's that coming from?

Do you feel you are entitled to be treated a certain way because of who you are, whether that's a boss or an administrator or something else? If you stripped away that identity, who would you be without it?

Visit the exercises for this chapter to understand and release more of your identities and be the true you.

Access the exercises through the membership site at http://tiny.cc/scl-member.

8. Masculine and Feminine

The concept of balance shows up several places in Soul-Centered Leadership. One of these areas revolves around masculine and feminine energy.

For whatever reason, our society has generally labeled certain characteristics of energy “masculine” or “feminine.” We’ll use this familiar terminology here, but that fact is that men have both types of energies, and so do women, and any examples we’ll use below could apply equally to women and men. The important point here is that when a person relies too much on one type of energy at the expense of the other, this can cause problems.

Masculine energy is traditionally considered action oriented, rational, direct, entrepreneurial, competitive, practical, risk taking, tough and assertive. Feminine energy is caring, intuitive, creative, receptive, nurturing and collaborative, and is feeling- and emotional-based.

When you are tilted too much one way, you may resent or resist some of the activities of the opposite polarity. For example, say you’re a female entrepreneur who is decisive, quick to act and competitive. These characteristics are drivers for much of your current success. But as a consequence, you may shy away from collaborative efforts or reject the thought of nurturing your employees. It simply might feel too much like “giving in” to allow these characteristics—the opposite of competitiveness and toughness—into the mix.

But the fact is utilizing all of the traits listed above can significantly strengthen your leadership. Not only is there a time and a place for competition and drive, a nurturing, compassionate hand to your team can be the ingredient that lifts your organization to greatness.

Both masculine and feminine energies, in a balance, are necessary to thrive.

In fact, to step into Soul-Centered Leadership, you need to master both.

As you read the following two sections, especially the one that relates to you, keep in mind that the **In Real Life** and **Exercises** for this chapter (like many others) have practical ways for you to implement in your own life.

Embracing the Feminine

If you're already materially successful, you've probably mastered the masculine. You've accomplished a lot and are great at setting goals, working hard, and achieving them. There may, however, be a good chance you've swung too far on that scale, and the lack of feminine energy in your life is causing issues both internally and externally.

It may be difficult for you to get along with people, or to form deep connections. You may have walled yourself off emotionally in order to push ahead. You also may lack creativity, or at least not have learned to harness it and see the greater possibilities that exist all around you. You may not have developed the ability to nurture yourself or others, and although you achieve your practical goals you may also lack inner fulfillment and peace.

This indicates a need to adopt a new approach in certain areas, which you can do by adding some feminine energy to your life. As we mentioned above, regardless of whether you're a man or a woman, you may resist so-called "feminine" practices like slowing down, connecting, listening, and being patient. You may even be proud that you don't engage in them.

I'm sure you've seen examples of how the overly masculine has sabotaged themselves. Consider for example Bernie Madoff, Pete Rose and Lance Armstrong. They were good at achieving, but at what cost? They were all on top at one point, and look how all their stories ended. I love watching Michael Jordan as a basketball player, but have you ever seen an interview with him? Does he really ever look like someone who is happy or has inner peace?

Entire companies can fall prey to the too-masculine trap. Look at the financial crisis. Enron is a good example. Toyota had the goal to be "the #1 car company in the world." They achieved it – by cutting corners, and at a great cost. Many large oil and media companies were on top of the world yet didn't nurture and create anything new. They just tried to defend what they had already; now they are falling behind.

All these examples illustrate that too much masculinity ends in a fall from grace, because you get so focused on the goal that you lose sight of other things that are equally or more important.

Bringing Masculine into the Mix

On the other side of the scale are the people too entrenched in the feminine. I meet a lot of men and women who have an idea for creating something—a business, book, blog, or so on—but it's obvious that their balance of energy is too feminine, and it's holding back them reaching where they want to go. It's one thing to be nurturing, receptive, intuitive, and so on, but unless this is combined with the more masculine movement into action, that book or business will be missing out on the force it needs to get out there.

If this is you, it's time to start taking risks. You need to get focused. Get determined.

You're probably turned off by people who show up with too much masculine energy. Perhaps you think they're too loud and aggressive; maybe you even use the word "ruthless" to describe them. But you're going to have to start putting a foot into that arena. It's your ego that's trying to keep you out. It's very comfortable and safe in the feminine.

Begin to cultivate the knowledge that you can walk into the unknown—maybe succeed, maybe fail. And start to be okay with that. Quit making excuses and jump in. I know it's scary, I know it's direct and blunt. It's also your path to growth. Otherwise you're going to stay stuck. It's time to change and grow.

There aren't as many stories of famous celebrities, sports stars, or companies operating with an excess of feminine energy simply because they don't have the "masculine" drive to be in the spotlight, compete, and focus enough to win. Remember, it's your nature to create, and creation takes drive, focus, and energy. If you have something valuable to offer the world, it's your duty to put it out there.

Coming into Balance

Developing whichever side you have ignored is the key to becoming a Soul-Centered Leader. One of my teachers once told me it's not that you want to strike a balance of 50% masculine and 50% feminine in your life. Your intention, to live holistically, is to bring 100% masculine and 100% feminine into your life.

Another trick I've learned is this: when you are learning skills on the other side of the table, you want to exaggerate them. In basketball, one shooting expert said that if you are shooting too far to the left every time, don't shoot for the middle. Shoot even further to the right. Then you will adjust yourself and make the shot.

It's the same with the masculine and feminine energy. Start focusing on the side that you want to develop. I can tell you now that it's going to be uncomfortable. The ego won't like it.

That's good. It means you're on the right track.

In Real Life

By this point in this chapter you probably have a good idea which energy is more dominant in your life.

If you're heavy on the masculine side and would like to bring more feminine into your life, try some of these activities with an open mind:

- Ask someone close to you for help on something you already know how to do, and just accept them helping you.
- Sit down and have a conversation with someone, and just listen. Ask them open ended questions and really hear what they tell you about themselves without interjecting your own ideas or trying to solve any problems that they bring up.
- Be okay without being in control. Go into a situation someone else is leading and be a great follower.
- Be okay to do something without being exceptional. Try just being average for a short period of time.
- Let someone else win.
- Dress in light colors.
- Tell someone you love them.
- Meditate silently for five minutes.
- Do or share something with someone without asking for something in return.
- Share a vulnerable feeling with someone.

To bring more masculine into your life:

- Take on a task you have no idea how to do, and be okay with winging it.
- The next time someone does something you don't agree with, confront them right away, even if you are emotional.
- Introduce yourself to someone new in a random place.
- Tell someone about a great accomplishment you've made.
- Take a leadership role when you normally wouldn't.
- Cold-call someone. Anyone.

- Make an inspirational speech.
- Play a sport that is you against just one other person, and have a goal of winning.
- Wear a dark, power outfit.
- Make a plan with specific to-do's and dates. Follow through on absolutely everything, checking off as you complete tasks.

Access the exercises through the membership site at http://tiny.cc/scl-member.

9. Letting Go

When there's something bothering you, you have four ways you can go.

1. You can **suppress** (or repress) the negativity. This is when you take those feelings and just bury them deep down. This includes being in denial – pretending the negative feelings don't exist – and projecting (covered in an earlier chapter), where you perceive and/or resent in others what you're repressing in yourself. This may be a great short term fix, but suppressed (and repressed, which is subconscious suppressing) can lead to all sorts of issues, one of which is health issues. In fact, a study by the University of Rochester and Harvard School of Public Health indicated that a significant number of participants who suppressed emotions may have been 70% more likely to get cancer over a 12-year period.
2. The second option you have is to ***express*** your emotions. You might have heard the general advice that if you're angry, let it out. You may do this through acting out or yelling. What really goes on with this kind of expression, however, is that when you bring it up and out it often gives more power to the emotion. This in turn can lead back to suppression and repression. It's like the ego is tricking you into thinking you've gotten rid of it.
3. Third is ***escape***. This is when you utilize a behavior to get you away from the feeling and thoughts you're experiencing. Drugs, alcohol, and any other addictive behavior, including excessive TV, work, sex, and exercise, are common escape routines. This approach, of course, only pushes whatever's bothering you aside—when the drugs or alcohol wear off, or when the work and TV run out, the problem's still there.
4. The fourth way—and the healthiest course of action (as laid out by David R. Hawkins in his book *Letting Go*, sounds simple but is quite powerful: ***let it go***.

Letting Go

Letting go is different from suppression. You can't simultaneously push something down and drop it from your consciousness. And it's different from expressing it. When you act it out, you own it more than you let it go. And it's different from running away from the problem. Because even if you run away from it, it's still there. And in all likelihood, you're afraid to look at it, to deal with it. Letting go of something means just that: letting go so that it's no longer an issue for you.

> ***Choosing to accept then let go of something is the quickest, easiest, and healthiest thing you can do.***

A form of Acceptance

The way you truly let go of something is to first own it and accept it—and be okay with it. You accept it without judgment. Feel the feeling. Tell yourself, "I am in this state, and I accept this." If you're sad, tell yourself that you're sad, and that's a totally fine state to be in. Sit with the sadness for a moment. Really feel it inside of you. If you have to cry, cry. Just be with it.

You can't skip or short this step; if you do, you won't have a strong enough hold on the feeling, so that when it comes time let it go you won't really understand or feel what you're releasing. But at the point where you're in acceptance and the feeling is present, simply have the intention to let it go. Then do just that: release it.

You'll be blown away by how often something just leaves you when you do this. Judgments, attachments, identities—all of these can be let go of in the present moment.

It's important, however, that when you let it go, you aren't attached to it leaving you right away. Some things will just disappear, and some won't. It's the intention of letting it go that's key; you're signaling to yourself that there's no longer any need to hold onto whatever the issue or feeling is. Not every single thing that you have gone or will go through in your life can be let go of right away. But a whole lot can be. And the more you practice this process, the more natural it will become, and the more you will reduce and eventually shed your negativity.

So, for example, say you catch yourself judging someone. You can say to yourself, "I am holding something against that person. And that's okay." Stay silent. Feel the judgment. Then tell yourself, "It's okay to let that go." Often times it will just flush right through you.

> ***Emotions are meant to be felt, then go away. It's your resistance to them that keeps them in your consciousness.***

When you release the resistance, the emotion doesn't have anything to hold onto.

As you get used to accepting your emotions – all of them – you can more quickly shift to a positive state. Say, for example, someone is angry with you. You might get angry back. But if in the next moment you can have the awareness that they're angry and that you chose an angry reaction in response, you can tell yourself, "Hey, I'm angry. Can I be okay with that and let it go?" Next thing you'll know you'll calm. And that will often calm down the other person.

Experiencing emotions is part of the human experience. Remember the chapter on Emotional and Spiritual Mastery? This is part of accepting all of yourself, all the time.

I'm at the point, ok most of the time, when if someone comes at me and is upset, even yelling at me, I know it's their issue, not mine. I stay present and calm and I know their upset doesn't have to do with me. They're just projecting it. Maybe they've had a bad day. Maybe someone they know is sick. Maybe they're under a deadline. Maybe they misunderstood what I did or said. Or maybe they're that way much of the time. But even that has nothing to do with me. That has to do with them and their own feelings about themselves. So regardless, I handle them with care and compassion, which instantly improves the interaction.

Choose your Response

I was in an airport one evening a few years ago and I found out that my flight was delayed. I wasn't sure by how much because different monitors were giving me conflicting information. I was tired and it was the end of a long day.

I went to the gate and saw two guys talking to the agent on duty. After waiting a few minutes for them to finish talking with her I found myself getting tired and impatient. I could also tell by their conversation that it might go on for a long time, because they obviously didn't fly much and didn't understand what she was telling them; they kept going back and forth on the same point.

I spoke over them, interrupting, and asked the agent, "Is the flight to San Diego still delayed?"

Well the one guy that was talking to her snapped. He turned around to me and started yelling about how rude I was, that I interrupted, and how he was an armed services veteran and he deserved more respect. It totally caught me off guard. I started to feel anger rising up in me.

Who is he to yell at me? I thought. All I asked was a simple question. What does him being a veteran have to do with any of this? It's not my fault he doesn't understand how to fly.

I came close to screaming right back at him. Then, I chose a different response.

I realized that it was late and that he was probably as tired as I was. He was obviously a little confused as well, because he didn't fly often and didn't know the drill when a flight was delayed or canceled. I took a deep breath and said, "You know what? You're right. It was rude. I apologize. It certainly wasn't my intention to upset you."

He turned around and stormed off. There was a guy standing next to me who saw the whole thing and said, "Man, he was the rude one. What was up with him?"

I thought for a second and said, "Maybe, but I really don't want one more thing to worry about." I was proud of myself. It was something that could have escalated very quickly, yet what would have been the payoff?

Sure, I got yelled at in an airport. So what? And sure, I could've yelled back. And we both know where that would have lead. Instead, I just simply let it go. And I was done with it and could move on with my night, rather than fuming and letting it take up more of my energy.

How many similar things do you run into on your average day that you hold on to, and which you could better serve yourself and others by simply letting go? In fact, what negative stuff are you holding onto right now that you don't need in your life?

Here's a hint: you really don't need to hold on to any of it . . .

The formula you can use is so simple. It can be used for so many things, and it's just three little words:

Let. It. Go.

In Real Life

The next time you experience upset or anger, take a slow breath and see if you can exhale the negative emotion and enter a calm state. Do it a few times.

What are you carrying around right now that you can get rid of? Own exactly what you're feeling, and then set the intention to let it go. Remind yourself that it's not serving you, and that it can actually be that easy to release it.

Visualize yourself as a spiritual being having a human experience. Remember that your core is a loving, compassionate soul. Anything else is just made up and is easy to let go of. Tell your Ego "thank you" for protecting you, but now it's time to be free.

Go through the exercises to work on your letting go process in greater depth.

Access the exercises through the membership site at http://tiny.cc/scl-member.

10. Reframing

Viktor Frankl was an astonishing and unique person. He was an Austrian neurologist and psychiatrist in the 1940s. He was also Jewish. This landed him in three Nazi concentration camps during World War II.

It's estimated that in Auschwitz, one of the camps he was a prisoner in, the Nazi's mass executed 800,000 to 1,500,000 people using gas chambers and other means. What makes his story so remarkable, so amazing, is that Frankl looked at his time there through a psychiatrist's eyes. He took it on as a study in human behavior after making up his mind to take something positive for humankind from his horrific experience.

And he did. He realized that the only thing you can't take away from someone is their ability to make a choice. Their freedom to choose.

> "What was really needed was a fundamental change in our attitude toward life. We had to learn ourselves and, furthermore, we had to teach the despairing men, that *it did not really matter what we expected from life, but rather what life expected from us.*
>
> We needed to stop asking about the meaning of life, and instead think of ourselves as those who were being questioned by life—daily and hourly. Our question must consist, not in talk and meditation, but in right action and in right conduct.
>
> Life ultimately means taking the responsibility to find the right answer to its problems and to fulfill the tasks which it constantly sets for each individual."
>
> (*Man's Search for Meaning*, Frankl, V., Beacon Press, 2006. p. 77)

In one of the largest human rights disasters the world has ever seen, he found the beauty. Whether it was in the smallest amount of generosity from the guards or a family giving their last scrap of bread to an orphaned girl, he found and celebrated humanity.

He ended up making it out of that camp alive, and his subsequent book, Man's Search for Meaning, was voted by the US Library of Congress as one of the top ten most influential books ever written.

It would have been easy for Viktor to think of himself as a victim, as a walking corpse just waiting to get his number called, but he didn't. He declared he would use the experience to benefit humanity. That's called *reframing*.

Reframing is when you look at a situation differently - through a new frame.

When things are tough, think back to Viktor. Here's someone who was in one of the worst places that the world has ever seen. And he managed to see it differently.

What about your situation? How can you reframe your situation? Reframing helps you take ownership and choose a powerful response. It's one more technique in the arsenal that you're building, another path to a fresher and more optimistic way of engaging with life.

- Industry headed towards a downturn? Great, it will weed out your competition and may lead to some acquisitions.
- Going through a divorce? Okay, that means you've been in an unhealthy relationship, and soon you'll free up energy and space in your life.
- Lose a key employee? Super, now's your chance to upgrade the position and bring in new energy.

If Viktor Frankl can do what he did in a concentration camp, surely you can do the same in the office.

Shift your Mindset

Reframing can go hand-in-hand with judgments. What are you judging negatively? How can you see that in a new frame? Remember, judgments are self-created, and so too is the frame through which we choose to look at a situation. By the same token, reframing can shift you from feeling like a victim to being an owner. It can also free you from attachments and identities.

One of my companies was particularly special to me because I had built it from nothing to become a big player in the industry, and I had been the CEO the whole time. It was my "baby." I had big attachments to the company, and my identity was tied up in it as well.

When I eventually sold it, the terms of the sale were such that I would be paid out over a few years. Halfway through that period, the company ran into issues, because of which I didn't get my full payout. This really bothered me. In my mind, I was entitled to that payout. I had a lot of anger against the people who had bought the company. I believed they hadn't performed as well as they could have, and I caused a lot of upset in my life around this.

After a while, I got tired of carrying that around, of looking at it through the old frame, so I worked on reframing it.

I realized that the company had given me so many benefits throughout my life. Through starting, running and selling it I had learned a tremendous amount. It provided me with money, experience, and status. And I had had a heck of a lot of fun doing all that. And of course, I did get paid out—just not as much as I was originally expecting.

I changed my viewpoint and freed up a whole lot of energy in the process.

Reframing almost sounds too easy to work. But it does work. I often walk people through the process and get very quick results. You can do the same for yourself.

In Real Life

Soul-Centered Leaders are optimistic and uplifting. What's going on that's negative in your office right now? How can you point people in a more positive direction?

The next time you find yourself in a challenging situation, take a moment to reflect. What's the most effective, conscious lens you can look at the problem through? Is there a way you could shift your perception to see what seems to be "bad news" in a different light?

Look at the exercises for this chapter for a process of reframing.

Access the exercises through the membership site at http://tiny.cc/scl-member.

11. Vulnerability, Authenticity and Integrity

I'll tell you what kind of leader people don't naturally follow: the ones that appear perfect.

If you've ever met someone who's achieved a lot in life and thought, "I should really like that person . . . but I just don't seem to connect with them," there's a reason. It's because they're so buttoned up that they're only showing you a highly controlled, "stylized" version of themselves—the picture they think the world wants to see. You only get to know the parts of them they want to show you. You never get to know them. On some level, we are of aware of this when we interact with those individuals, only to feel disconnected and out of touch with them.

They're afraid to show you anything but their positive side. They never admit that they have doubts, fears, or failure. Everything is always great with them...on the outside. Though on the inside, they're human, just like the rest of us. Oddly enough they lack confidence. They fear that if they show anything but the perfect them, they will be rejected. Since they crave acceptance from others, this drives their behavior.

Take it from me, I used to be one of those people, and every so often, I still can be now. I do it when I'm under pressure and intimidated. Maybe there's someone who I look up to. When I get around them I want them to like me, and I react by putting up my guard; to only showing the "acceptable" me. And that often creates a disconnect between us.

I know – it's tough being vulnerable! It was difficult for me to write that last paragraph. But I wanted to be an example.

> ***Connections, intimacy, and therefore loyalty, are achieved through vulnerability.***

It takes courage to bring that vulnerability forward, especially in a business setting. Too often it's equated with the idea of weakness. But you need to be vulnerable to be a Soul-Centered Leader. And there's a healthy way and an unhealthy way to be vulnerable. Throwing up all your fears and insecurities is not the healthy way. Being truthful and heartfelt is.

People have good intuitions. If you're not vulnerable, they're never going to trust you, even if they're not quite sure why they don't. And without your people's trust, you're not going to be an effective leader.

Earn Respect and Loyalty

I was working with a business owner who was having a bad quarter after many years of success and growth. His industry was down, and he was about to have a quarterly meeting with his staff. It was difficult for him as he never had to worry about cutting back before now.

I said to him, "What are you going to present to your people?"

He sighed. "I'm going to tell them everything's great, so they don't lose faith."

"Is that true? Is everything smooth sailing right now?"

"No," he said, looking downwards. "Things actually aren't all that good."

"Do your people know that?"

"Yes, of course. The whole industry's down. It's impossible not to see that."

"So, then, what do you think the people are going to think when you tell them everything's great?"

After a few moments of silence, he got it. "They won't believe me. They'll think layoffs are coming and I just don't want to give them the bad news. They'll probably start looking for new jobs."

I nodded. "That's what I would do if I were them. What's more, they won't believe anything else you say, either, if they know you're not being upfront with them about this."

What we did from there was work out how he could be neutrally honest, how he could tell the truth, yet not sound like he's looking for pity or bringing negative emotions into the situation. He could sound like he was—and actually be—simply giving them the facts.

He ended up going into the meeting with all this in mind. When he started out by addressing the fact that they had to cut back and start retrenching, everyone felt a sense of relief, because he brought it out in the open.

He laid out his plan forward to his people, which was based on an accurate assessment of the state of the industry and their position. He asked for their help to get through this without laying anyone off; which he admitted he couldn't even guarantee. Everyone got onboard, and it was a rallying cry for banding together.

It turned out that he did better in the downturn than any of his competitors. His company ended up with more market share and ultra-loyal employees, and even allowed them to buy up two other companies who didn't handle the downturn as well.

His honesty and vulnerability were the turning point—by being straightforward even when it was difficult, he earned the trust, respect, and loyalty of his staff.

Embrace Your Truth and Integrity

Remember that as a leader, being vulnerable should be followed up by a way forward. In the above example, the situation was that their industry was slowing down. Their leader didn't just talk about the problem, he let them know the situation, got collaborative feedback, and executed on a well thought out plan.

Be careful: the ego doesn't like authenticity and vulnerability because they mean that it, and you, don't have total control of the situation. The ego feels its job is to be in control, to protect you. Opening yourself up can initially feel like it goes against everything it stands for.

The practice of authenticity, vulnerability and honesty at times requires you to have faith in the goodness of others and be secure with yourself, as people aren't going to respond in kind every time. For example, when it comes to employees, there are so many places where it's easy to let little un-truths slip in. During employee reviews, do you often give the highest mark possible because you have some fear about confrontation or hurting someone's feelings?

What about the next time you have to let an employee go? Rather than firing them abruptly, is there an option to working with them to form a transition plan over a few weeks that supports them while doing a smooth handover? How transparent can you be with your team and those around you?

These situations can be difficult. They can open you up to awkward interactions, epically as you start on the path of openness. Like many skills in this book, it gets easier-natural even-the more you do it. Look at how you go about these kinds of interactions. Really challenge everything that you think you have to hide. Often the benefits outweigh the risks.

When it comes to prospects and customers, how often do you make up little white lies? Little white lies often seem so small that when you lie you tell yourself, "It's so small that it doesn't matter"; which, of course, is a lie in itself...If you're late to a meeting, do you blame it on something or someone else even when it's because you simply left late? Do you inflate the size of your company or your accomplishments? When you negotiate with vendors, do you make up stories, maybe about pricing and terms from other vendors, just to see if you can get a better deal? And when you do things like this, do you tell yourself it really doesn't make any difference? Or do you just get a kind of rush when you exaggerate and get away with it?

I was guilty of many of these. For example, I would always add a few million to the size of our company's revenue, a few extra office locations, or a few more to the headcount. I would test the limits because I was addicted to the little rush of getting away with it. I'm pretty sure it never even mattered, yet I would always have a little fear that I would get caught. But all that energy I had wrapped up in the falsehood was wasted. When it's tied up there, it isn't available to be used elsewhere. And I'm also out of integrity.

The thing to remember is this: people can usually sense this. They may not know that you're out of integrity, that you're blustering instead of being authentic and honest, but they can often feel it, and that leads to a sense of disconnection with you. Being vulnerable doesn't mean giving away the farm in negotiations; it means being present, open and authentic.

People almost always respond positively to vulnerability and authenticity when they are expressed in a healthy way.

When it comes to the moment where you tell people your truth, do it in a conscious way. Prepare yourself beforehand. Go slow. Talk from your heart. Make eye contact. Connect.

Be you.

In Real Life

Be on the lookout for little white lies. What are you exaggerating, and why do you think you're doing it? Start being precise and honest about what you tell yourself and others.

Discover in your life where you have fear that someone will find out something about you that you don't want them to find out. Is that fear in an agreement or a conversation? Wherever you find it, consider the situation. Your fear of discovery is a good clue that you aren't in integrity on that issue. Fix it by coming clean.

Reflect on your life. Are there any relationships, duties, areas, that just feel out of place? What can you do to change them?

In the exercises for this chapter, find out where you are out of alignment and work a process to get back into integrity in a healthy way.

Access the exercises through the membership site at http://tiny.cc/scl-member.

12. Courageous Action

Leadership is a scary process. Think about it: you start out in a situation in which you're comfortable. You have a set amount of responsibilities and perform a specific range of tasks. You work hard to put yourself into a new position—for example getting promoted or starting a business. Then all of a sudden you have more responsibilities. You find yourself doing tasks you might never have done before, and now people are watching with a microscope to see how you do. Often you get little or no training or support.

Of course that's scary! But that's leadership. And unless you go in with the right mindset and tools, you'll start acting out of fear and insecurity, which leads to disaster, because once you go down that hole, it's much more difficult to climb your way out.

But here's a little secret: Everyone experiences fear, but no one likes to admit it. The fact is, if you don't experience fear, you're playing it too safe.

The definition of courage isn't acting big and audacious without fear; it's being scared and doing it anyway.

Remember how your true nature is to create? When you set out to create something great, you open yourself up to vulnerability and fear, and maybe even rejection and failure. What better way to deepen your self-compassion and continue your evolution than by recognizing this and supporting yourself through this scary process—which you yourself started? This is what builds up true confidence.

Understanding and Overcoming Procrastination

How many times have you had an idea for a book, a product, a company, that you were *sure* would work, but which you didn't follow through with? Maybe a position opened up but you didn't apply. Or perhaps there was a time where you could have had a conversation with someone really important, but fear grabbed you and you didn't engage them.

Swami Smaranandaji has said, "Inactivity is far worse than activity driven by the ego." Christianity even classifies procrastination as one of the seven deadly sins; they call it *sloth*. Let me state this plainly for you: Laziness is the most cowardly way you can go through life. It's the ego playing it totally safe and not risking anything. You don't evolve and grow by sitting on the couch and hiding.

Think back at your life and see all the opportunities that have passed you by. Don't beat yourself up over them; simply acknowledge honestly that your ego has been holding you down when it comes to new adventures, especially ones that involve putting yourself out there.

Now imagine how many other people in the world face the same challenge. What if everyone had a tool to recognize and overcome this resistance? What would the world look like then?

See how much this one simple skill of overcoming procrastination is needed? If you're reading this book, that right there means you are better than most at taking that first step. Take that and build on it.

When you accept your role as a leader, you're accepting responsibility. The buck stops with you. Others are watching and relying on you.

You've probably forced yourself to move forward in uncomfortable situations many times in your life. But what if you didn't have to force yourself? What if it didn't have to be uncomfortable? What if you had a greater understanding of this from a psychological perspective, and when you felt the fear rise up, you knew why it was there? Then you could push it out of the way and move forward. Would you be more successful? Would life be easier for you?

Let's go back to when you are an impressionable little kid, say around five or six years old. There was only one thing your world revolved around: the love and adoration of your parents. It didn't really matter what you had to eat, what toys you had to play with, or anything else. As long as mom and dad (or whoever was rearing you) showed you love and affection, there was a feeling that everything was right in the world.

Say your dad was really hard on you. He did this because he

wanted to "toughen you up" and get you ready for the "real world."

Imagine back then you're in a race with a hundred other kids. Your dad's at the race, encouraging you on. And you come in third. Pretty good, right? But what does your dad say?

"Son, why didn't you win? What's wrong with you? You didn't try hard enough. Pump your arms more and put your heart into it."

"Ok, Dad," you say, not as excited now about taking third and wanting your dad's approval. So the next race comes, again against a hundred other kids. You race as fast as you can, pump your arms as hard as you can, and come in second.

Is your dad happy? No, he's angry.

"You suck," he says. "Second place–that's the same as first loser. I'm disappointed in you."

Knowing that the love and adoration of your father is the main thing you care about, what do you think happens in your impressionable mind?

You make the connection that winning equals love. If you win, you will get the love and affection you crave. If you lose, if you get anything other than first place, you aren't good enough. In fact, you may never be good enough.

You just have to keep fighting, fighting, fighting.

Here's another example: a few weeks later you come home having received an A+ on your math test. What does your mom say?

"Son, an A+! You're perfect...I love you so much!"

Here again you make the same connection: perfection equals love. But you only get love when you get 100% right. So you learn again that you always, always have to strive for perfection. Or it's not good enough.

But then the next time you have a chance to take a hard test or an easy one, which are you more likely to choose?

The easy one, because if acing it will give you love, the easier test gives you a better chance to be perfect.

If the choice is between an easy test and *no* test, which will you choose?

No test.

Because there's no chance of failing if you don't take the test. And *that* is the root cause of procrastination. You don't start things because there's no guarantee they'll turn out perfectly. This, too, is where the drive to be a perfectionist comes from. At some level deep within yourself you perceive that anything but absolute perfection will cause you to be further removed from love and affection. And since absolute perfection is, to put it mildly, hard to come by and impossible to guarantee, what's the point of even trying?

New Definition of Success

The way to overcome your procrastination, fear, and resistance and move into action is simple: Change your definition of success.

Instead of having success equal perfection—which, as you learned above is what is causing you not to move forward—have success now equal taking action. Play in the game, and make sure that you're all in.

See, courage is found simply in taking action. Give up on the notion that you're going to start on something and have it come out perfectly. If you don't get started you stay stuck in the swamp of fear, anxiety, circular thinking and more.

Yes, it's a little ego game (we're still using terms like "success" and "win"), but it works. Really, really well. In fact, you can take this process a step further and frame your action as an experiment. Because remember, with an experiment the only way we can't succeed is to not try. So calling your courageous action an experiment takes all the pressure off.

The Honest Truth

I once met a referral contact from networking for coffee one day. The woman was in a similar industry, and there was a possibility we could refer each other business. We had what I thought was a regular enough meeting where we learned about each other both professionally and a little personally. When I got back home later there was an e-mail from her to me, basically telling me she didn't like me and she wasn't too keen on getting back together. (She said it more nicely than that, but I got the message.)

For a few hours this really affected me. I thought, with more than a touch of bitterness and confusion, What do you mean she doesn't want to get to know me better? Doesn't she know who I am?

I replayed our entire conversation, feeling hurt (playing the victim), looking for anything I had said that might have offended her.

Finally I took a step back. A thought had broken through the fog of self-doubt and irritation: Not everyone I come across will like me. I used to have this belief that everyone should like me and want to be my friend. Implicit in this belief was the feeling that it was important for my self-esteem for everyone to like me. Seeing this was actually a great gift. When I truly took it in, it was like a great weight was lifted off of me and I could become more myself.

The truth? I have a strong personality. I do a lot of good in this world. And there are going to be some people who are drawn to me, and some other people with whom I don't connect. And that's totally okay.

These days I'm aware of this. If I meet someone who doesn't seem to be enjoying my company, or I get strange vibes from, I simply move on to someone who I do connect with. I don't take it personally; it's just information. And this has opened up a whole new world for me when I'm out with strangers. When I see someone new, I go up to them and say hello. If they don't seem like talking, I simply move on. And when I do talk to people, instead of trying to get people to like me, I'm more myself. Which, funnily enough, makes me more likeable!

Do you see what went on here? Instead of having a goal of getting people to like me, of having that desire drive my actions, simply introducing myself to them became the victory. Now each new person is an experiment unto him or herself. They don't have to like me. And by the same token, there are some people that I like and some that I don't. And that's fine too. I meet some people who seem very well meaning and kind—yet for some reason I just don't enjoy being around them and I find myself getting triggered when they're around. The best way I can describe it is that our energies don't match. I've learned to recognize this, honor it without judging these people, and simply choose not to engage with them. As I said above, it's about information. Sort of like whether I like broccoli or not—if I don't, it's not because there's something wrong with broccoli. I just don't like it. (For the record, I do like broccoli...)

There have been so many times in my life when I've put off conversations that I perceive will be difficult or uncomfortable. In my software companies I would occasionally get very large prospects or potential partners that I would put off calling, or not call at all, simply because I was afraid. Afraid they would have an interest and that when I got in front of them I would embarrass myself, get rejected, and maybe even be laughed at. I've put off firing people because I knew it would be uncomfortable. In the past there have been festering problems in my organization that I've known about but didn't want to address, because I knew it would lead to a confrontation. Not all the time, mind you, but those situations did exist.

The problem is that when I give in to this reluctance, without fail it holds my organization back in some way. It represents a lack of Soul-Centered Leadership on my part. It's also only postponing the inevitable; most problems simply can't be run away from.

Perfection means Playing It Too Safe

You might be thinking if my goal isn't to come in first, will I lose my motivation? Will I get complacent?

No, you won't. That's part of being all in. When you play you do play to win. You just don't get too attached to it.

As both a competitor and a risk-taker, when you start playing in bigger and bigger games–trying riskier and more courageous actions–you are going to challenge yourself. You just have to be ready to not win all the time. When you don't come in first, or aren't perfect, you need to praise yourself for your effort. Have fun with it. Enjoy the journey. Be present. Learn as you are doing. Drop all your expectations, attachments, and identities. Tell yourself that you aren't going to judge yourself on the outcome.

When I was a sophomore in college playing basketball, I was really proud because I was shooting 79% from the field (regular shots, not free throws). This means that if I shot 100 times, I would score 79 times out of that 100. Normally anything over 50% is good, so my percentage looked astronomical. As a young player, I brought this up to the coach, bragging a bit. He looked at me and said, "That's because you aren't shooting enough."

I knew he was right. I would only shoot when I absolutely knew I would make it. I was holding my team back because I wasn't taking other shots that I should take—out of fear that I would miss them. That fear was stronger than the chance that I might actually make the shot.

We aren't meant to be perfect. By doing more, you'll learn so much more and develop skills and resilience you never knew you had.

Can you imagine what your world would be like if you could apply the tools you're learning here each and every time you encounter resistance and fear? If you totally eliminated procrastination from your life? It's all possible. You just have to do the work, do the exercises, and learn the skills.

This chapter taught you the origin of procrastination, fear, and resistance. Self-Limiting Beliefs will go deeper into understanding them as well as giving you a way out, and the chapter on self-worth will take you the extra mile.

In Real Life

What are you putting off? What's on your to-do list at the beginning of the day and still there at the end? How can you turn getting it done into an experiment—something to try for the sake of learning?

Catch yourself when you're striving to do something perfect, and be imperfect on purpose. That's right, get used to not being perfect. Also resist the temptation to tell anyone about it or make excuses. If they notice, great, just accept it.

Do something you wouldn't normally do without any attachment or expectations except to learn. In fact, have fun with it. Instead of trying to "win" or be first, play with it. Experiment. Have fun in your own way.

The next time you call a prospect or meet someone new, tell yourself that the truth is they may or may not like you, and that's okay. In fact, you may or may not like them as well! Just show up with a positive, upbeat vibe, say what feels natural, and let the conversation take the course it takes.

What are you doing really, really well? How could you do it at a higher level? Are you doing it really well because you're playing it safe? Test yourself. Take it up a notch, but be careful not to put yourself under a massive amount of pressure to be great at it right away. Be okay with not being awesome at it at first, and see what you learn.

Go through the exercises in this chapter to change your way of thinking and move into action with ease and grace.

Access the exercises through the membership site at http://tiny.cc/scl-member

Part III – Life Integration Skills

In the first part of this book you were introduced to basic spiritual and psychological concepts. The second part taught more direct, powerful techniques to help you work on different areas of your life. This third part wraps up those concepts and techniques into a set of profound, holistic principles. These principles incorporate everything you've learned so far, in service to giving you what you need to effect major change in your life and the world.

Recall the five-line model. As you've been moving through the book, you've been working on deeper and deeper levels. Now you're going to be working on the Authentic Self, or soul level, which affects all the other levels and is by far the most powerful.

It's where the real fun begins.

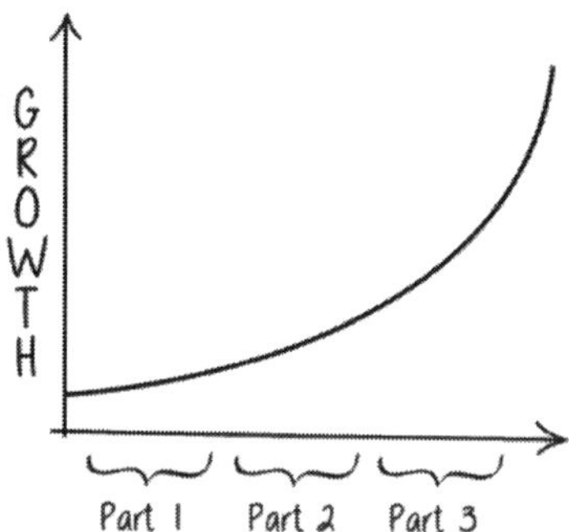

Self-Limiting Beliefs: Origins

Self-limiting beliefs are just what they sound like: beliefs¬ that hold you back. They usually exist on the unconscious level so you don't even know they're there.

> ***Identifying and releasing yourself from a self-limiting belief is one of the most freeing actions you can ever take for yourself.***

Bear with me, as they may take a little while to understand. It's worth it though so hang in there.

To get a sense of where in your life you might find limiting beliefs, ask yourself these questions:

Do you find yourself driven to work all the time?

Does it sometimes feel like you attract drama into your life?

Do you experience a lot of guilt?

Do you make self-sabotaging decisions that hold you back?

Are you so goal-oriented that you live your life always chasing the next achievement?

Are you searching for a more stable, loving relationship with your spouse / partner / kids?

Have you hit a plateau in business? In life?

Are you constantly busy and harried?

Do you wonder what it's going to take before you're happy and truly fulfilled?

If you answer "yes" to any of these questions, it's probably because you have subconscious beliefs at work inside yourself. Don't worry, you're in good company: we *all* have such beliefs. The trick is to bring them into the light of day—and then let them go, which you are about to learn how to do right here.

Since limiting beliefs usually exist on an unconscious level, you may need to dig around to uncover them. You may find some that you grew up with or adopted somewhere along the way, whether they came from your parents, your cultural or religious background or someplace else. Let's start by looking at the variety of places where self-limiting beliefs come from.

(A tip for going through this chapter and the next is to take notes while reading. Print out the exercises now, so you have them next to you. There will be many examples of where these beliefs show up. Every time something rings true to your life, make a note of it. That way you'll have a head start on the exercises and you won't forget anything for later.)

Intergenerational

The number one place you get your behaviors and beliefs from is your family. Mother and father have the greatest impact on the beliefs you pick up as you grow up. We call these Intergenerational self-limiting beliefs.

It's estimated that up to 80% of your behavior has been passed down from mom and dad, both through your genes and how you were brought up; nature and nurture.

Before we get into discussing how to go about changing some of these beliefs and behaviors, keep in mind that a great many of them (in this category and the others) are very valuable. For example, I was taught—both consciously and via modeling through my parents' behaviors—honesty, the importance of giving back, hard work, and many other great qualities. I'm thankful these traits are part of my family's lineage.

It can be helpful, too, to remember that this is not an exercise in digging up the past and figuring out who to blame for what's wrong in our lives. In many cases, the beliefs we pick up, particularly from our parents, reflect their concern for us. In other words, even though we learned limiting beliefs from them, in most cases their intentions were to give us what they thought we needed for life. Sometimes that backfired, and we took away beliefs that now hinder more than help us.

And keep in mind that although these are things you inherited, every single belief and behavior can be changed. Don't use your past to justify being a victim in the present. Simply focus on the beliefs that are holding your back and engage the processes you'll learn in this chapter.

Take some time now to really reflect on your family.

What were your parents' attitudes towards work? Money? Love?

How does that relate to you? How you react to situations now? Your beliefs?

The more you look at your own life through the lens of the way your parents reared you, as well as in the light of other significant interactions, such as those you had with relatives and other influential people in your youth, the more you will see connections with your beliefs and behaviors today. Sometimes these connections are obvious and sometimes they aren't. It may be, too, that certain attitudes and beliefs are expressed a little differently in your own life than they were in your parents'—but those beliefs are still there just the same. (There's a complete process at the end of this chapter to draw them out.)

If your parents were always worried about money, which may have created a state of constant tension around the house, how does that line up with your beliefs and actions now? I've met plenty of wealthy people who could never make enough money—no matter what they had in the bank. They always plowed forward with a quiet (or not so quiet) desperation. The fact that some of them had more than enough to retire on—and certainly more than the average person—meant little in the shadow of their limiting belief about there "never being enough money."

The two most common reasons for people having this belief are either 1) their family had a fear of being poor and destitute, or 2) their parents hammered into them that no matter what you have, it's never enough – you always need more. So more often than not it's this unconscious, irrational belief that they are just a step away from the poor house that haunts them.

Sometimes people have such a fear of what their parents went through that they go to the other extreme. For example, if someone had a mother who was always embarrassing herself, the child may work hard to make sure they never embarrass themselves in public. They may take this to an obsessive degree, so much so that they feel inhibited in public and end up missing opportunities because of this. What's more, they may also judge people who make a spectacle of themselves in public, whether intentionally or otherwise. This is a form of projection; they are seeing the person as they saw their mother.

Based on what your household was like growing up, what decisions did you have to make as a child? Maybe you had an overbearing father, and as a little child you were conditioned to always be quiet and not draw attention to yourself; otherwise you might get yelled at. That may play out now as you often don't speak up when you have something valuable or important to say. It may make you afraid to stand out from the crowd, and again keep you from jumping into the fray when an opportunity presents itself.

What really bothers you? What fears drive you? Find out what your behaviors are and start mapping them back to your family. It will be eye opening. As you uncover these patterns, you will have some profound realizations. Have the intention to be kind to yourself as you start to dig in and change these subconscious beliefs. Don't judge yourself or get down on you or anyone else in your family. This is a process of self-realization and ascension. Go through it with compassion, kindness, and love – for all involved.

Racial / Cultural / Geographical

Another significant area from which limiting beliefs can arise is comprised of racial, cultural and geographical influences. These may be broader than the boundaries of our immediate family, but together these influences form a kind of "super" extended family. We often draw from them at least a portion of our identity.

Consider, for example, what behaviors are "normal" for your race? How about people from your home town? Do you come from a "conventional" middle class town where long hair and tattoos were virtually unheard of—except for those "roughnecks" who lived just outside city limits? Maybe you were raised in a culture where an unwed teenager who became pregnant was shipped off to live with relatives in a distant town while she had her baby. And if you grew up in the American South, you probably encountered a different set of values from someone who grew up in Los Angeles or New York.

On one standardized test, a set of African Americans did worse when they were asked the question, "What race are you?"[1] Another group of African Americans taking the exact same test—excluding only that question—performed better. This indicates that they had a subconscious belief that negatively affected their mindset around their race—and it affected their proficiency on that test.

When we identify ourselves with a group of people, a race, or a culture, we can often unconsciously play into our hidden beliefs about them. I'll give you a few specific examples from my own life at the end of this chapter.

Religious

Sometimes stereotypes are simply beliefs we buy in to. For example, my family is Catholic, and guilt is a common theme. Jewish people might joke about how their fellow Jews compete to tell you how bad their life is. "You think you have it bad? You should see how bad I have it." In certain religious systems, women are treated differently from men. And consider how many religions embrace the concept of martyrdom, where having a tough life can be seen as a kind of honorable suffering.

I'm not saying that all Catholics are guilt ridden, or all Jews complain. Nor do I think any religion has "cornered the market" on guilt or complaining. I also don't believe that every member of a particular religious belief system subscribes to the stereotypes of that system.

What I'm saying is far simpler: We often play into the stereotypes of the religion we grew up with, in the same way that we are influenced by our families and the cultures of which we're a part. So if you're Catholic, look at your life. If you happen to feel a lot of guilt, realize that life doesn't have to be that way. If you're Jewish and you tend to complain to others, is that a stereotype you play into, something you took upon yourself from your religious background? If so, stop. It's not fun being around you.

It's not my intention to say that stereotypes are true, but they

---

1 https://www.brookings.edu/articles/the-black-white-test-score-gap-why-it-persists-and-what-can-be-done/

often have some basis in reality. They aren't just made up. What's more, we often play into them, consciously or unconsciously. They can be used as a kind of shorthand for relating to one another, as excuses for feeling a certain way, even as humor, though often of the self-deprecating kind. They don't have to arise from religious beliefs either, as we've seen above. If you're from New York, for example, you might find yourself talking with a "tough guy" accent in certain situations, or justifying aggressive behavior. Or if you're the oldest in the family, you might catch yourself thinking everything's your responsibility.

Remember, these cues are really clues—information to help you to look at your life with a caring, neutral eye, in service to clearing anything that is not the absolute truth. The aim of these exercises is not to judge yourself or the background from which you've come. Rather, it's to free yourself from what's been holding you back. Once you've managed to clear these beliefs that aren't serving you, what's left is your Authentic Self.

Gender

Male / female limiting beliefs are alive and well. We touched on this concept above when we talked about masculine and feminine energy, and how our society has assigned specific characteristics to these types of energies. Of course, something similar happens with actual men and women. Males often feel pressure to be strong, stoic and unfeeling. Many hold the belief that emotions make them look weak. Females, on the other hand, often feel that they are judged by their looks, their weight, or the femininity. Women may tie their self-worth to these traits.

Personally, I have to work to be vulnerable and share my feelings. It takes intention and effort to overcome a belief that as a man, I shouldn't ask for help. I know, too, that women often have to overcome subconscious judgments by others. This no doubt contributes to the "glass ceiling" phenomenon, and to the wage disparities many of them encounter. It's been shown, too, that unconscious teacher biases account for the reason that a greater percentage of males develop higher math skills than females, even though there's really no actual underlying difference in math ability between the sexes.[2]

Event / Situational

You may undergo an experience—often a traumatic one—in your life that causes you to create self-limiting beliefs in order to protect yourself. Such events can include sickness or injury, abuse, and parental arguing (especially when you're younger). Other types of trauma, for example getting kidnapped, witnessing a murder, or even something as seemingly objective as severe weather (for example, being caught in a hurricane) can leave a mark. You may, for example, avoid arguments—even constructive ones—if you were caught in the crossfire of your parents' arguments when you were younger. You may feel more than a little nervous around sick people if poor health plagued your childhood. Or maybe you always rush to play the caretaker, even at the expense of your own health. The rumble of distant thunder might put you on edge if years ago your house was flooded in a powerful storm. Whatever the case, our subconscious minds often imprint certain rules in our heads in an effort to protect us—even when such beliefs and practices don't serve us at all, and don't even make logical sense any longer.

I can't stress enough how important it is to not *judge* any of these beliefs—or yourself for holding them. Understand them as information. And I know we're touching on some very deep subjects, things you've carried with yourself perhaps for your entire conscious life. So as you do start uncovering them, remember to have compassion for yourself. As we've seen, so many beliefs are passed on to us from previous generations, or via religion, race, gender, and through other influences. Up till now there was little we could do about it.

Now we know better, and so this is the time to practice acceptance and compassion for yourself as you look towards freeing yourself from the beliefs that are holding you back. Remember, too, that there is always more help available to you. Reach out to a professional or contact me and my firm. We're always here to give you

---

[2] http://www.apa.org/monitor/2010/07-08/gender-gap.aspx

guidance on how to work at deeper levels, heal faster, and get to a better place.

Here are two examples from my own life, and there will be many more in the coming chapter, where we go into the most common beliefs.

A woman in my family nags a lot. One time I asked her why she does it, and she answered, "Because that's what the women in our family do!" This is an intergenerational, cultural, and gender-based belief. And she has no intention of changing it. This belief is now part of her identity, and she's fine with that.

My intention isn't to judge her. This is how she chooses to be. It can be difficult for me to accept this at times because I want the best for her, but that's out of my control. It's just my job, in this situation, to love and accept her.

I grew up in Pittsburgh, Pennsylvania, which, when my parents were kids, was a big steel mill town. The people in their neighborhood were all blue-collar immigrants or kids of immigrants. People either worked in the steel mills or in small businesses supporting the mills and the community. It was so blue-collar, my parents told me, that sixty or seventy years ago, no one in their town would trust someone wearing a business suit. A suit represented the bosses at the steel mill, or perhaps someone in the government or from another large company.

Here, then, is a cultural and geographic belief at work. Imagine growing up in that environment and one day having to wear a suit. Do you think you might experience some inner conflict, that you might have a sense of unease or self-consciousness that you couldn't quite understand?

If you did get offered a job that required you to dress up, you might even self-sabotage the whole thing. That would be your subconscious' way of doing what it thinks is right, and protecting you.

In Real Life

You can start being very aware of how your consciousness changes around different people or groups. Does your energy change around co-workers, family, different friends?

As you observe different people in your life, see what sticks out. How do they talk, what do they focus on? How does that relate to you? When you're with them, how do you act differently?

The exercises in this chapter ask you deep, reflective questions geared to help you uncover the beliefs at play within you. In addition, keep in mind that your answers to the questions here will help you in the next chapter.

Access the exercises through the membership site at http://tiny.cc/scl-member.

Self-Limiting Beliefs: Types

Now that we've examined the origins of our self-limiting beliefs, let's look at the most common places they show up in our lives. Keep in mind that these beliefs come in all shapes, sizes, and variations. I'll say right off the bat that I've had each and every one of these, and there's a very good chance they'll be familiar to you too.

Since self-limiting beliefs exist on an unconscious level, you may read about them here and initially not think they apply to you. Even the exercises may not fully bring them out. Then a day, a week, a month later, it might hit you; you come up against a belief that's been dogging you your whole life, and once you make the connection it feels like you've opened up a whole new avenue for growth in your being.

That said, a note of caution; when you start to uncover your beliefs, you may realize that some of them are what's been driving you to succeed. For example, the first one we'll look at, which equates work with success, is very common. When you run up against one like this, you may think to yourself, "Sure, I want to heal, but I also want to stay successful." Because of this it's common to want to hold on to a belief out of fear that if you let it go you'll lose your edge.

I can tell you that's absolutely not true. As you let go of these beliefs, you'll actually become much stronger as a person and as a business leader. You'll start to live from the true you, and when you do this you tap into a power and energy you never knew existed. Releasing yourself from self-limiting beliefs is like freeing yourself from chains that have been holding you down for years. You'll start punching through the areas in your life where you've been stuck—areas you might not have even known you were stuck in, or dead ends you'd given up on the possibility of ever escaping.

So let's get started.

Self-Limiting Beliefs: Work = Success

The number one belief I find that holds people back is this: You must work hard to be successful.

Now don't get me wrong—hard work can often lead to success. But most people think that they have to go hand-in-hand; success only comes with hard work.

That sucks. Personally, I want to be massively successful – without a ton of work. Doesn't that sound like a better option? A prime example of this is when I built up my software company so that it had strong middle management. It was providing me with consistent cash flow, and it only required that I work around ten to twenty hours a week.

But I simply couldn't accept success like this. I felt guilty that others were working long hours and taking on so much stress while I was making a significant amount of money with minimal effort. So I found unnecessary projects to do around the office, with the result that I was there fifty hours a week appearing as if I was working, but really not doing much of value.

Take a step back and look at this picture: I had achieved the "holy trinity" of entrepreneurship: a self-running business that was profitable and growing and which didn't require me to manage it. But my beliefs and patterns didn't allow me to enjoy it. Crazy, huh?

Yet absolutely true.

Many, many of us have this belief, especially when we come from lower / middle class / blue collar families. Often our father, and sometimes our mother, got paid by the hour. Farmers, factory workers, armed services vets all are great at drilling this belief into their kids. You can't succeed without hard work. The belief may even go so far as to say it's somehow not "real" success unless you've worked hard to get it.

But while a strong work ethic is great, it can be misunderstood. It can create the belief that we aren't deserving of success unless we work hard. In this equation, your self-worth is tied to how hard you work. (Remember how I mentioned that you tie so many things to your self-worth?) One consequence is that when we have a measure of success we subconsciously think it's our duty to become a martyr – someone who attains success only at deep personal cost.

This creates an unhealthy relationship with us and an unbalanced life. In my own case it led me to work more than I had to simply because I was successful. Imagine the same belief operating in a parent who could be spending time at home with family instead of wasting away hours on busy work at the office. This belief can put you under unbearable stress, turning you into a "workaholic" who wonders how to make time for family, relationships, or health—convinced that your company needs you too much to stay away. You'll have time for that "other stuff" later. But later never comes, because you get addicted to the workaholic lifestyle, a habit you also wear like a badge.

This behavior can also become a form of escape. Maybe you work so much that you don't have to deal with a romantic partner, a difficult relationship, kids, family, your health, or something else:

- I can't make it to the family event, honey. You know I always work Saturday mornings.
- I don't have time to exercise. I'm in Atlanta today, LA tomorrow, and New York the next.
- Sure I miss my kids, but this work isn't going to do itself, and I have to pay for college somehow.

Consider some of the other ways this belief manifests itself in our lives:

- Do you feel that you can't lead someone unless you've worked your way up from the bottom?
- Do you find it hard to respect someone in authority if they haven't done your job or come from where you have?
- Do you feel guilty because you go on vacation, or don't work as long hours as others, or have to miss work to go to a doctor's appointment?
- Do you look at someone who's successful, or who has maybe won the lottery, and think, "They don't deserve that?"
- Do you believe that "There's no free lunch!" or "If it's too easy, it can't be true!"?

Take a good look at yourself if you answered yes to any of these questions. Chances are good you've got some version of the "you have to work hard to succeed" belief operating within you. But guess what? Sometimes things do come easily. Sometimes you even get a gift from the universe. In fact, it's pretty great when that happens, though if you don't believe it can happen, it sure seems to happen a lot less.

Another way that the Work = Success belief holds you back appears in the variation where you think that if your company becomes more successful, it'll create more work for you and you won't be able to handle it. So it's more comfortable to keep working in the zone where you know you can be successful; this can lead you to subconsciously self-sabotage potential future successes.

I found this belief holding me back in my own life. When I was running my software companies and we had an important sales presentation with a prospect, I sometimes had a nagging thought that if we got the project my life would take on a whole new degree of stress. Combine this with my need to control everything—if my company grew more, how could I stay in control of it all?—and I was in a situation where, without realizing it, I was holding my organization back from growing. I plateaued at the point where I could still keep my beliefs, but I wouldn't let myself grow beyond them. Looking back, I'm sure that I subconsciously sabotaged deals because I was already overloaded and didn't want to take on the extra perceived burden. Could you be holding yourself back in the same way?

Can you picture yourself successful and yet not working hard? I'm not talking twenty years from now. I'm talking today. Can you imagine great success right now, with a relaxed life? Because you know what? You deserve it. And it's possible. Drop the belief that Work=Success and be open to the idea that success is possible without killing yourself or ruining relationships to get it. A new path is there for you, and it's amazing.

In Real Life

Start tuning into yourself during work and when you're supposedly "off the clock." Do you ever catch yourself feeling guilty? Where is that coming from? Do you often feel you need to be working harder even after you've put in a long day? Do you find yourself doing busy work at the office just to tell yourself and others that you're "hard at work"?

When something comes up in your non-work life that you know you will enjoy, make it a priority.

Start setting clear boundaries at work as far as when you will and will not work. Share them so your team can respect them. (While you're at it, if you're aware of members of your team who push themselves more than is good for them, consider exploring these ideas with them as appropriate; in the long run a better overall work/life balance will only help you and your team be more productive.)

Do you find yourself glamorizing or bragging about working long hours? Start doing the opposite: work fewer hours and get excited about that. Set appropriate daily goals for yourself, and when you're done, stop working and do something uplifting, whether by yourself or with family or friends. See how that feels.

To start retraining your subconscious that it's possible to give up this frantic business, take a few minutes each day to close your eyes and imagine yourself calm, working a manageable schedule, and achieving even more success.

Answer the exercises questions in order to open up to greater success with much less effort.

Access the exercises through the membership site at http://tiny.cc/scl-member.

Self-Limiting Beliefs: Success Trade-offs

If you become successful, what do you expect that to "cost" you in your life? What do you think you will have to give up, trade, or endure in order to become successful? These are interesting questions. When I teach this in a class or workshop, many people's first answer is "nothing", only to have a life-changing revelation by the end.

The belief here has to do with sacrifice, i.e. what do you have to sacrifice in order to have success. In order to succeed, you have a subconscious agreement that you have to give something up.

Here's another personal story to illustrate this concept. My father was an entrepreneur, and because of his work he was often absent, and our family life suffered. Keep this in mind as I tell you about my sister.

She and her husband bought a retail pharmacy. At the time she was juggling kids and work, and she was happy because they were doing better than expected for their first few months in business. But something was wrong. We were on the phone one afternoon and I noticed that when she started talking about her family she sounded a little down. After a little exploring, it was clear that she had become resigned to the fact that her family life was suffering because of this new business.

I stopped her and asked "Ami, you do realize it's possible to be doing well in your business and to have a happy home life?"

There was a long silence. Finally she said, "Michael, I just realized I never thought that was even possible."

This is an example of how deeply ingrained self-limiting beliefs can be, and why it's so important to shine the light of awareness on them. It had never even occurred to Ami that there was another way. In her mind, the conflict between a happy family and a successful business was almost a law of nature.

Now a little later we're going to get into a powerful process showing how to reverse self-limiting beliefs, but for now I will point out that sometimes just by realizing we have them we can let them go and free ourselves up to engage with life in a new way.

Remember that these are subconscious beliefs. Look at past patterns and see where they show up in your own life.

A woman from Romania once heard me speak about these beliefs at an event, and we sat down to talk a week later. She explained to me that her family holds an intergenerational belief that if someone becomes successful, they'll get sick. Not cold or flu sick, but cancer and leukemia sick. She went through a list of her family members and offered example after example drawn from her family tree where, when individuals became successful in business, they followed this up by coming down with life-threatening diseases. Can you see how simply having that belief could affect your life?

Beliefs show up in different ways. Do you think that because you're the boss, you're also the one who always has to take on the dirty jobs? Or if someone has to work the weekend, you think it's your duty to do it? Does the captain always go down with his ship? Do you always have to be the one to make the sacrifice and "do your time"?

There's a word for people like this: martyr.

Are you waiting for something to happen before you can feel happy or successful? Then you have this belief. Do you ever look at wealthy and successful people and get jealous? Maybe you think they must have inherited their fortune or had to lie and cheat or sacrifice their family life just to get it, and that's why they're where they are—and you're not. I used to find myself jealous and resentful of wealthy people for reasons like these. I felt if I was going to be successful I'd have to compromise my own ethics.

This was a pure self-limiting belief. Eventually I realized that I would never become wealthy with that mindset.

Of course, it's not necessarily a bad thing to work weekends now and again, or to pick up the slack for the team. Just as in the Work=Success equation, it's not that work and success aren't related. Similarly, there are times when it makes the most sense to forego something pleasurable in order to get something done. It's the energy you have around the decision that counts. If you often say things like, "Ah my life sucks. I'll cancel all my plans for the weekend and get this proposal done." that's you playing the martyr. That's you thinking you need to "pay the price" for success. I did this for years, and looking back it wasn't necessary, and it held my company back.

No more though. It's unhealthy, not fun, and it caused me a lot of suffering.

Obligation. Duty. Sacrifice. These are all words that, in certain situations, can have victim and entitlement undertones. Good news! The only thing you're a victim of is this self-limiting belief, and now you can let it go and get on with your life.

In Real Life

Start tuning in to your thoughts and beliefs. What do you feel you have to give up in order to be successful? What do you think is unachievable for you as far as family, health and happiness go, if you continue along your current path towards success?

The next time you have something you want to accomplish and think, "There's going to be a lot of hard work and sacrifice involved," take a minute to enter into a short meditation. Envision your goal and be open to the fact that you may get there faster and more easily than you ever imagined. Don't try to convince yourself; simply be open to the possibility.

Do you find yourself doing the dirty jobs or working hard, then acting like people owe you or should hold you in higher regard for doing those things? Do you hold it over their heads in some way? That's ego. Move to a Heart-Centered place and work from there. Consider the possibility that you take on these things for your own reasons, perhaps because your own particular self-limiting beliefs make you feel you must.

Where are you playing the martyr in your business or personal life? What are you doing out of a sense of obligation that might not really need to be done? What do you perceive your "duty" to be? Challenge those beliefs and see what happens.

If you hear about someone who got lucky or achieved something with little effort and find yourself judging or resenting them, change your mindset. (This exercise can also work if you think of people you already know who "struck it rich" more easily than you think they should have.) Remember: luck and successes aren't always earned. Sometimes they just happen. Be open to these things coming to you, and be happy for the people who have already found them.

Access the exercises through the membership site at http://tiny.cc/scl-member.

Self-Limiting Beliefs: Lack of Worthiness

A friend and I were talking one day, and in the course of our conversation she brought up how she hates it when people are arrogant. I thought for a second, and then said that while arrogant people aren't my favorite either, what really gets me is when people don't own their power, when they don't accept the gifts, skills, and abilities they already have.

How many people do you know who are great at something, yet who downplay it, and don't move forward with it in their lives? Maybe they have an amazing idea for a business. Maybe they're excellent at playing an instrument, or maybe they're really good with people. These things and more, when creatively put into action, could move their lives forward in many ways. But they play small when the world needs them to play big. They lack a sense of their own value, of their own inherent worth.

It's time for all of us to start bringing our best to the world.

We can see this play out in so many areas. For example, when someone compliments you, do you tell them why they're wrong?

When someone says "great job,", is your reply "nah, it was no big deal," you reply. "It was the team, not me." "I just got lucky." "I'm blessed."

Or do you look them in the eyes and say a sincere "Thank you"?

It is okay – healthy even – to be confident and secure with yourself. This is different from arrogance. It may simply be the fact that you are great at something. This doesn't make you a fundamentally better or worse person than anyone else, but if you happen to play piano particularly well, or have made some exceptional and strategic business decision, or something else that deserves praise, why not just accept it?

Michael Jordan is great at basketball. That's a fact. If you were to say "MJ, you're awesome, thanks for all the great years," wouldn't it be awkward for him to say "No, I'm really not that good. It was mostly my team"?

So where might you be doing this in your own life? I mentioned that becoming a Soul-Centered Leader is about building up your self-esteem. Hiding from your worthiness moves you away from that. Being honest about your gifts, skills, and abilities brings you closer to who you are. It is, in fact, a matter of integrity – with yourself and with others.

There's a story that's told about a doctor who retired to a small, rural town. He didn't tell anyone he was a doctor as he didn't want to stand out. Least of all did he want anyone to think he was bragging, so he kept his former profession to himself. Not too long after he arrived a young girl next door became ill. The family was poor, and they couldn't afford to travel to the nearest doctor. Of course, they didn't ask their neighbor for help; they didn't know he was a doctor. At the end of the story the girl dies because the doctor didn't take ownership of what he was.

This is a parable, of course, but I'm sure you get the point. I've seen talented person after talented person pass up opportunities simply because they weren't confident enough to say, "Yes, I can do it."

If you were put in a group of strangers who needed to form a team and they asked what you were good at, what would your answer be? And what would go on within you internally when they asked? Anxiety? Fear? Pay attention to that. What you feel in response to these kinds of questions offers a clue to how you can heal and come into a more loving, compassionate, authentic relationship with yourself. You may even discover that you've been hiding your talents from yourself.

A big growth moment for me came when I participated in a leadership event several years ago. We had been put into groups of eight people and each group sat at their own large table. Many of the people at my table were older and ran larger companies than I did, and none of us knew each other. The facilitator told each table to choose a leader. We started by awkwardly glancing at each other. One of the guys started to point to the oldest, best-dressed gentleman at the table to nominate him.

Even though I was nervous, I raised my hand and said, "I'd like to be the leader."

They all shrugged and said "Okay, sure. So I took the helm. I have no idea whether I was the best leader at that table or not. It doesn't matter. I stepped up. And even if I wasn't the best leader, how was I going to learn to become a great leader by sitting on the sideline?

I was very proud of myself with that little action on that day.

Another example came when I facilitated a YPO (Young Presidents Organization) Forum Retreat. This was a group of eight CEOs and owners, two of whom ran businesses that had over $2 billion a year in revenue. I had them do an exercise where they had to come up in front of the group and, with open body language and a straight face, say, "I am a powerful business person."

Most of them expressed huge resistance to doing this. Some of them really fought it. One participant was convinced he wasn't a powerful businessperson. I had to remind him that his revenues were in the billions.

Another person said that there were way better businesspeople than him out there. My response to that? I told him I wasn't asking him to say that he's the best businessperson in the world—simply that he's powerful.

What was happening was that the participants were, for the most part, using this feeling of unworthiness to drive them. It's like they were being chased by a fear of not being good enough to stand out, so they had to keep running away from the opportunities that came their way.

But really, they were running from themselves, from their own worth. The truth is that they—and you, and me—will never feel truly happy and fulfilled until we change. we will always feel like frauds, and we will be haunted by the fear of discovery. In fact, when I do one-on-one or small group work with very successful people, one fear that almost every person confesses to is that they feel like a fraud. A fraud to their co-workers, peers, and often most of all to their families. There's so much pressure to be successful, and they admit that sometimes they really don't know what they're doing. Life feels out of control, they're winging it, and deep down they're scared to death that it will all unravel at any moment.

As I say, this is an extremely common fear, and what tends to happen over time is that people develop defense mechanisms to deal with it. For example they never let anyone close to them because they're so worried that someone will "see" that they're not perfect and in control. They live their lives in comfortable relationships that lack intimacy. This can lead to drug and alcohol use, as well as to addictive behaviors.

Until you address the unconscious belief of your "lack of worthiness," you're a prisoner.

When we put ourselves into new positions of leadership and responsibility, all of a sudden, we have new levels of responsibility that we most likely haven't experienced before. And normally we don't get much if any training or support; we're on our own. Of course that's going to be scary.

So we try to control everything. This, of course, is impossible. Sound familiar?

When I found out that this is common, that I'm not the only one who questions themselves, has fear that things might collapse, and that I'm feeling that life is sometimes out of control, I immediately felt relieved. I thought everyone else had it all figured out and I was the only screwed up one!

No, we're all dealing with our own stuff. The funny thing is that it's really all the same, only no one knows anyone else is going through it because we get so good at faking the appearance of having everything under control.

So take a deep breath. Know that you aren't the only one; not only that, you're normal. And you're on the right path. Just keep going.

In Real Life

When people compliment you, practice accepting it. Even if you don't believe you deserve it, for some reason they do. Look them in the eyes, and simply say, "Thank You."

Make a list of your strengths and abilities. When the opportunity arises for you to share your talents in these areas, step forward and offer your services. Do it with neutral energy, not in arrogance or shyness. Just be factual and straightforward. Then relax into the situation and see what happens.

When you have fear about being a fraud and aren't sure what to do, make a list of your accomplishments to date. Tell yourself you didn't know what to do then, either, but you persevered anyway—just like you'll do this time.

Pretend you have to make a big speech. The person introducing you wants you to write a short bio listing all your accomplishments so that the audience knows to whom they are listening. (You can pull this out to help you with the point above as well.)

Be aware of those areas where you are holding yourself back and making excuses. Some of these excuses may sound like "I'm not ready," "I'm not old enough," or "I don't have enough experience." When you see a healthy opportunity and these sorts of thoughts rise up within you, go for it anyway and see what happens. Even if it doesn't work out the way you want it to, the victory over the self-limiting belief comes when you simply step into action.

Access the exercises through the membership site at http://tiny.cc/scl-member.

Self-Limiting Beliefs: Perfection = Success

Perfectionism. Oh, yes. That insane drive to do everything perfectly. Chances are that when you read this section's title and that first sentence, you chuckled, because you see it so clearly in your own life.

Now keep in mind that this belief, just like all the others we've looked at, can and likely has been of benefit to you in your business life. It's great to have drive, to shoot for quality work. The focus to have things be "perfect" is often what sets us apart from others and enables us to create great things.

Left unchecked, however, perfectionism will make you insane and drive others away. Like everything else in your life, you want to be mindful of how you work with this aspect. Is striving for perfection causing you stress? Do you beat yourself up when you don't perceive yourself as perfect?

If so, that's what you want to let go. Perfectionism can be a never-ending cycle. It drives you to create success. You achieve your goals, and then take on more and more—always with the expectation of perfection. But when you realize it's not possible, you freak out and then *burn* out. Maybe part of your life falls apart, your business takes a hit it didn't have to, you go through some drama in your life—and then you start all over again.

There are two ways in which this belief that Perfection=Success shows up.

The first is in the incessant drive to be perfect. Are you never satisfied? Do you dwell on the one or two things you didn't execute flawlessly instead of the many, many great things you *have* accomplished—regardless of whether or not you did them perfectly? Are you happy and content right now? Or are you not allowing happiness and contentment into your life because something feels somehow "out of place"? Clinging to the belief that you'll be happy once things are "perfect" is a recipe for *un*happiness. Because how many times in life have you experienced something truly perfect?

The other way in which Perfection = Success shows up is when you *are* successful and you make an agreement with yourself that you must do everything in your life *perfectly*. It's like you constantly have to *earn* your success through perfection. This tendency can be a little harder to identify, but once I learned about it myself, I knew that I carried that belief, and that it was quite powerful in me.

When things were going well, I had this determination to have everything in my life work out in perfect order. That would cause me to stress over things I had no business worrying about. I noticed that when I was doing very well at work I would get fanatical that everything in my life should go as planned. When I had a sales presentation, I would stress out if our team didn't do *exactly* what we had laid out ahead of time. Anything that didn't go as I meant it to would gnaw at me.

If someone went off script, I would fume inside. I would start wondering things like, *What are they doing? This isn't what we talked about. Do they know what's at stake? I'm going to kill them! What else is this going to affect?*

I was obsessed with controlling everything and creating a perfect presentation. This is, of course, impossible. But that didn't register with me at the time. I didn't roll well with changes, and since I was always preoccupied with control, I wasn't present and connected. Small changes to the plan would throw me off my game and I would resent whoever I thought caused the change.

This was a very tough way to go through life. There are so many things that can happen in life that it's impossible to plan ahead for. In this sense, expecting perfection is a flawed and *im*perfect approach. Holding yourself to an impossible standard in such situations will make you less flexible, and this might cost you more than a "perfect" execution is worth.

Perfectionism *can* lead to success. But massive success, and true fulfillment, comes when you can move forward when things aren't perfect. When you open yourself up to the fact that facing unknown circumstances is a part of life, what you're really doing is *trusting* that you're up to the challenges. You won't always win, but even so-called "perfect" plans don't always bring the results you want. But you will learn to trust in yourself that you can handle things on the fly. And you will develop trust in the universe and an understanding that at the end of the day, no matter what happens, you'll be just fine.

In Real Life

Practice being imperfect; the next time you get dressed up to go out, ruffle your hair, wear mismatched socks, or put on colors that don't go together. Be okay without being perfect, and have fun with it. The next time you catch yourself beating yourself up, tell yourself one (or more) of the following things:

- Yes, correct: I am not perfect this time, and there will be many similar times after this one in which I am not perfect.
- Looks like my higher power is giving me another sign that I'm loved whether or not I'm perfect. Thanks for the reminder!
- Is that all I messed up? Shoot! I thought there'd be more . . .
- Yup, the funny thing is that I didn't do that right—and yet I still kick ass.
- I'm a risk-taker; I do an incredible amount of things, and it's inevitable that I won't make the grade sometimes. But if I don't make mistakes, I'm playing it too safe.
- That's right, it wasn't perfect, and that's my new way of doing things. So I'm right on track.
- Perfectionism: I do use you to do a lot of things well, but I'm going to give myself a break on this one.
- Okay, that wasn't exactly right, but the things I did do well are . . .
- You know what? I'm awesome anyway.
- Ah, well. So be it. On to my next task!

When the anxiety of something not going to plan strikes, put your hand over your heart, be very still, breathe in and out smoothly, and just concentrate on your breath. Give yourself permission to be joyously imperfect. Feel the tension lift as you free yourself and prepare to move forward.

Access the exercises through the membership site at http://tiny.cc/scl-member.

Self-Limiting Beliefs: The Independence Curse

Almost all boot-strap entrepreneurs share this particular belief; it accounts for many of the "lone wolves" and self-declared rebels out there. It usually expresses itself like this: "I'm better off on my own. Others hold me back."

I've met entrepreneurs who could make a million dollars with a partner but still not count it as it a success – because they didn't do it on their own. These individuals are so fiercely independent that they run away from collaborations or teams they aren't leading themselves.

Does any of this sound familiar?

- Do you resist asking for help?
- Do you work hard not to show any weakness?
- Do you have a burning desire to do things "on your own terms," even to the point where you reject input from experts or other authorities?
- Do you have issues delegating? Do you make everything run through you because you don't trust others to make the right decisions?
- Are you the person who always takes the other side of an argument because you always know a better way?

If so, you've probably had success in small areas doing things exactly your own way. Because you're really smart, can quickly pick up new things, and work with intense focus, at the end of the day you'll find a way to make things work. But here's the rub: you use all your reserves of brilliance and resilience to outwork and overcome the fact that you aren't open to help.

Even when you try to work with others, you probably get frustrated more easily because you don't perceive them to be as smart or as dedicated as you. More to the point, you may feel they simply don't think the same way you do. So rather than spending time bringing them up to speed you convince yourself it's easier and more efficient to get rid of them and do it solo.

It's easy to burn bridges this way. When you get defensive and exclude or cut other people off, you miss any chance of connection with them. Anything that they were going to bring to the table—new ideas, new opportunities, new relationships—all vanish along with them. In short order they grow to distrust and, frankly, dislike you. This is one of the reasons why people who are overly independent often have trouble connecting and having intimate relationships with others.

Again, your independence, drive and resilience are gifts. They have no doubt served you well at many times in your life. But if what you're reading here resonates with you, you're overusing them. Your need to be independent is holding you back personally and professionally, keeping you from the truth that the world is full of new ideas and possibilities that often come to us through other people. Not only that, but if you're trying to do every job that needs to be done because you can't trust anyone else to do it, I can guarantee you're missing out: you simply can't get it all done and stay open to new possibilities, much less enjoy yourself.

There's a much better way to go through life.

Soul-Centered Leadership means being open to other people's ideas. It means truly listening and working with others. You don't have to fight to be the smartest person in the room all the time. In fact, it's great when you come to others and admit that they know more than you. Doing this allows you to learn from them. Moving forward and making changes almost always requires connecting with other people, sharing and delegating the workload, exchanging and brainstorming plans and ideas, and creating the synergy essential to long-term success.

So drop this shield you've created around yourself. If you want to be a strategic leader you have to empower others. How are you going to scale up your business if you're the only expert in everything? If anything, that attitude is a surefire way to keep things small—only as big as your own skill set and limited time will allow. Instead, find people and firms that know how to do things better than you. Lead them, or accept their input and move forward. Don't try to reinvent the wheel at every juncture.

Remember, too: People don't expect leaders to know or do it all. What they do expect is that their leader can show them the way to the solution.

And this is what can really happen when you reach out and work with the proper people, form conscious partnerships, and allow great things to happen.

In Real Life

Go to someone who reports to you. Ask them to show you how to do something. Sit there, patiently and engaged, as they give you direction even when they're telling you things you already know. Then simply thank them.

Look at an area of your business that isn't working well. Find someone (most likely outside of your organization) who knows about this area. Ask them their opinion about the situation and just listen as they share their thoughts with you. Really listen; this doesn't have to be just an exercise—they may in fact offer you the solution to your problem. Use what the Buddhists call "Beginner's Mind," where you pretend like you're learning what's being offered for the first time (and perhaps you are). See if you take away something from the conversation that you had missed because you were thinking you already understood the situation inside and out.

Access the exercises through the membership site at
http://tiny.cc/scl-member.

13. Affirmations (Overcoming Self-Limiting Beliefs)

We're just about ready to look at how to overcome the beliefs that have held us back. But before we do, let's recap what we've learned so far.

Now that you've begun uncovering your beliefs, can you see how they may have become the norm for your life? This is how they work; some part of us accepts them at a bedrock level deep within us and they become as natural as the scenery in our lives. We simply don't question them, so they continue to influence us. But once you start exposing them to the light of day, things begin to change.

Working with these beliefs is necessary in order for you to reach the heights that the universe has in store for you. They've been holding you back like an invisible collar wrapped tightly around your neck. Now that you realize this, you can release the collar and run free.

The Value of Beliefs

Keep in mind, once again, that these beliefs likely did serve you after a fashion in the past—or at least they served the individuals who passed them on to you. For example, perhaps your father really did have to work hard to support your family. Maybe there were times when you had to take on the lion's share of work in order to meet a deadline. In other words, there have been times when acting on these beliefs was necessary and actually supportive. They may continue to have some benefit in your life today. Our goal is to bring them into the light of day so that we can use them consciously, rather than having them rule us from behind the scenes.

Again, hard work, when engaged from the Authentic Self space, has great honor in it. Very few amazing things have happened without someone working their butt off. Beliefs and behaviors can serve us, but we also want to be open to miracles, to new ideas and new ways of doing things. The universe has a way of showing us shorter ways to greater success. By keeping the drive for hard work and success while dropping the belief that you have to work hard for success, you'll have the right mix of traits to thrive and live a heck of an easier life.

The same holds true when you shed the belief that success comes with some other kind of difficulty. Your universe expands and the quality of your life increases. Opportunities start to come from seemingly everywhere, and things just become easier.

We also talked about how some of our beliefs may have been "hand-me-downs" from our parents or grandparents, our culture, religion or race, and so on. It's important to realize that these sources have also passed along great, supportive qualities. What do you hold dear in your own family? What may they have taught or handed down to you that you still value today? The importance of compassion, work ethic, intelligence, family bonds?

Just like it does for your race, culture, geography, religion, and gender; there is so much connection, bonding, community, and strength available in these areas. Have you had any mentors or role models? What have they taught you? Remember to honor everything that came out of these connections, even though the beliefs that you carried with you may no longer serve you and must now be let go.

What's amazing is that when you do identify and heal a self-limiting belief that's been in your family or community for years, you don't just heal it for yourself—you do so for every subsequent generation in the future. At least, you set the wheels in motion for others to follow suit. You become a role model, and just by being you, you show others how to let go and live a more elevated conscious life. What greater gift can you give your whole clan?

You Are Worthy

When you step into worthiness you begin to feel your true power. Do you think the universe blessed you with talent just to have you shy away from greatness and play small? Be honest and true to yourself. Know what you're capable of, and be proud of it. Most likely you've worked to develop and hone your own unique skills, and it's okay if you are naturally gifted or enjoy yourself. Don't be shy. Own it. Really. That's your duty to the universe. Own and use your talent. Then flourish.

Use your perfectionism, eye for detail, and drive when they fit the situation. They are all great assets– necessary, even – in this world. Just check in with yourself and be aware of when they threaten to take over. Have them work in service to you; don't let them drive the bus.

It's wonderful, too, to be a freethinker, to be courageous and try new things.; to not put yourself in a box but instead to test limits and traditional thinking. That's where innovation comes from. Just remember it's not you against the world; let the world support you. It's a giving place, and so are the people who share it with you. Let them in, hear them, and accept help. Then see how far you fly.

Affirmations – Path to Freedom

Now that we've looked at these beliefs in depth, it's time to move out of them and into freedom.

Think of self-limiting beliefs as nothing more than habits. How do you change a habit? By creating a new way of doing things—then repeating it until a new habit is formed. We use this method to overcome our self-limiting beliefs by first becoming aware of the belief, and then creating an affirmation to shift our beliefs and actions in a different direction. An affirmation is a powerful statement that cancels out self-limiting beliefs and teaches us a new way of being.

Affirmations have the following characteristics:

- They start with "I am . . ."
- They're stated in the present tense, as if they're happening now (even if you haven't yet fully achieved the desired behavior or situation).
- They affirm the truth that addresses and reverses the self-limiting belief.
- They are powerful, uplifting, and stated in positive terms.

Examples:

- I am working thirty or fewer hours per week in my business and am exceptionally effective; we continue to grow at a rapid pace. (addresses Work = Success)

- I am enjoying a successful marriage, a thriving business, and working out regularly, leading to a healthy, happy life. (addresses Cost of Success)
- I am attaining great abundance both in monetary wealth and success, and I know I'm worthy of this success. (addresses Lack of Worthiness)
- I am very productive and take risks, sometimes failing, often succeeding, always learning, knowing that I am a great creator. (addresses Perfection = Success)
- I am gracefully working with colleagues and receiving feedback from them, knowing that others hold a key to my growth. (addresses The Independence Curse)

Post, Read, and Integrate

Once you have written down your affirmations, go to your mirror every morning and look yourself in the eyes. Repeat your affirmation until you feel it . . . you know it . . . you are it. Let it sink in. Some days it may only take saying it once. Others it may take ten minutes of repetition. But don't leave that mirror until you believe it.

Some people post their affirmations on their steering wheel, on the home screen of their phone, on the wall in their bathroom—anywhere they are sure to see it at least a few times a day. Hey, whatever works! The more you can integrate these affirmations into your life, the more you will change your patterns and beliefs. What's most important is that when you read your affirmations, you take time to really have them soak into your consciousness. Don't simply repeat them rote while you're thinking of other stuff you have to do that day. Feel it as real.

Affirmations can be a little tricky to nail down, especially at first, and getting the wording just right is very important. If you've registered for the Membership Site, you've been given an invitation to our Members Only Facebook Group. If you would like me to review your affirmation, post it in the group. Make sure you describe the exact self-limiting belief you're overcoming, and I'll help you tweak and wordsmith your affirmation to address it.

In Real Life

After formulating your affirmations in the exercises, find places to post them so that you're reminded of them several times a day. This will not only help you remember to repeat them at a conscious level; it may also help them become a "background" part of your life. When you start taking these new beliefs as givens, you'll really begin to soar.

Say – and feel into – your affirmations at least twice a day.

Go through the exercises in this chapter to create your affirmations and be on the way to freeing yourself from these beliefs.

Access the exercises through the membership site at http://tiny.cc/scl-member

14. The Hero's Journey

You might have heard of Joseph Campbell's concept of "the hero's journey." It's become more and more popular over the years, and with good reason: it's a powerful, profound idea that touches most everyone on some level. What's nice for our purposes here is that it fits perfectly with the idea of Soul-Centered Leadership.

But before we talk about that, let me give you some context and background about the hero's journey. Joseph Campbell was a psychologist and religious scholar (some call him as a "mythologist") who studied under the legendary psychologist Carl Jung, himself a student of and collaborator with Sigmund Freud. Campbell studied every major religion as well as countless myths and fairy tales, and what he found was that they all followed the same story arc. He called this "the hero's journey."

Now you see aspects of the hero's journey reflected in just about every movie, TV show, and book out there. In fact, when George Lucas read about Campbell's work, he hired him to be an advisor and re-wrote Star Wars to follow the trajectory of the hero's journey, which very likely help explain why the movie became lodged in the imaginations of millions.

The reason the hero's journey has such power is because it's so universal. It strikes a powerful chord within all of us, conveying a fundamental aspect of human experience.

Here's a simplified rundown of the basic elements of the hero's journey (with references to the original Star Wars in there for fun):

1. **The Reluctant Hero** – The story starts out with a "reluctant hero." Someone who is just a regular person, but who gets unwillingly thrown into a dramatic or adventurous situation. (Luke Skywalker started out as just a farm kid, remember?)
2. **Call to Action** – There's a calling for the Hero to do more. (Obi-wan asks Luke to join him and learn about the Force.)
3. **Refusal of the Call** – At first the Hero-To-Be doesn't want to answer the call. Perhaps there's something comfortable about the familiar life they're leading, or they're afraid to risk the dangerous path ahead. (Luke at first declines Obi-wan's offer, instead choosing to help his uncle on the farm.)

4. **Taking the Leap** - The Hero is thrust into the action, often through a combination of events leading to a choice they must make. (Luke's foster family—his aunt and uncle—are slaughtered; not only is there nothing left for him, now he also has a motivation to fight, which he chooses to do.)
5. **Allies, Enemies, Tests** – The Hero meets allies (R2D2, C3P0, Han and Chewbacca), and enemies (Darth Vader, the Empire), and faces many tests (infiltrating the Death Star).
6. **Despair** – This is the time when things look the bleakest. The Hero is out of options; survival seems unlikely at best. Often this is where the Hero faces their "Shadow Self," that which they fear the most. (The treacherous Death Star trench, where it seemed impossible to precisely target just the right spot to blow up the Death Star in time. Darth Vader, and Luke's own fear and initial lack of trust in himself, is Luke's shadow self.)
7. **Finding Courage / Transformation** – The Hero surrenders the old way of thinking, trusts in themself, and overcomes their greatest flaw, which leads to transformation. (Luke, guided by Obi Wan Kenobi's voice, puts away the targeting computer and trusts in the Force.)
8. **Climax / Overcome Shadow** – The Hero defeats their shadow self and is victorious. (Death Star explodes – yeah!)
9. **Crowning of the Hero** – The once reluctant Hero is celebrated and gets recognition for their courage. (Luke and his friends get their medals from Princess Lea at the medal ceremony)

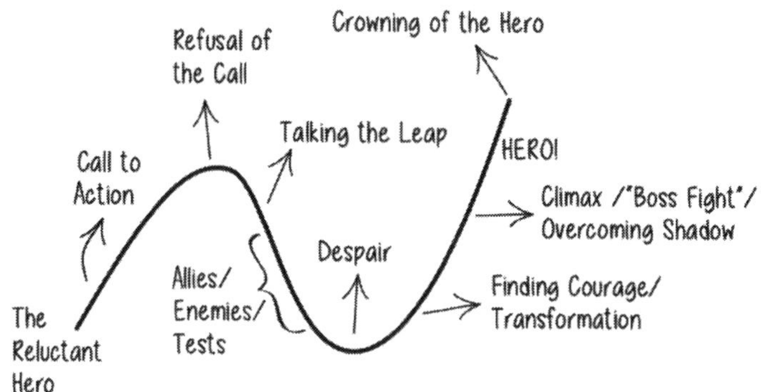

Go ahead, play with this idea; it will help bring it to life even more. Take the last movie you've seen – action, romantic comedy, animated – and run it through the steps above. Of course, if it's a romantic comedy the Hero's challenges will be different. Rather than a naïve farm boy, Darth Vader and a Death Star you may have a dorky office worker, a mean boss, and a comically awful office situation. But even if the "victory" lies in capturing someone's heart, you'll still find that the Hero is transformed along the way. Maybe they learn to love themselves, stand up to their boss, find a new job—and so become the person who wins the guy or girl. Try it yourself with your favorite book or movie and you'll probably see pretty quickly how well the ideas match up. The template of "the hero's journey" has been around since the dawn of time. It exists in the stories our ancestors told each other around the campfire as well as in the tales of Shakespeare, The Wizard of Oz, and countless others

The reason "the hero's journey" resonates with us so much is that it's the story of us.

The Story of Life

And it's not just in stories. We can often find this same pattern at work in our business and personal lives. As a Soul-Centered Leader you'll start to see the hero's journey play out all over the place. And you can use its template as a powerful way to reframe whatever's taking place.

For example, think about it in the context of creating a business. There will be variations on the theme of course, but for the sake of simplicity, consider that when most people consider a new venture they may be reluctant to dive in, because it usually involves a sacrifice of money and time. When they finally take the plunge, they're bound to encounter enemies, allies and tests—the kinds of obstacles that made them reluctant to start in the first place. They run up against one too many challenges—maybe they run out of cash—and in a moment of despair consider throwing in the towel. They press on, continuing to educate themselves, and find what they need to succeed. Things turn around and they're off and running.

In fact, we can see patterns like this, big and small throughout our lives. For example, imagine a typical sales cycle. A prospect comes in and you get excited (call to adventure). You learn a little more, and maybe you don't think they're such a good fit after all (refusal of the call). Then the more you engage, the better they look, and you start a relationship (taking the leap.) When it gets close to decision time, they look like they're getting cold feet and the deal's going to fall through (despair.) Then, just when you think you may lose the deal, it ends up closing, and you're the Hero.

The same pattern runs through our relationships, whether they're with romantic partners, our children or friends. For all these reasons, we can truly say: "the hero's journey" is the story of our *lives*. That means *your* life, too.

Yes, you are that Reluctant Hero.

Your Hero's Journey

You've had ups and downs in life. You're probably happy about the ups and judge about the downs; all those failures, tough times, difficult parents, breakups, the abandonment or abuse—whatever it was for you. You think, "Why did that have to happen to me?"

What you may not realize is that when you have down times in life, that's part of what makes you *you*. When you mix those with the positive in life—love, caring, accomplishments—you get your *personality*. You develop character and resilience, and you get your strength and general kick-assedness. In other word, that's how you earn your Hero status.

How does a muscle grow? By straining it to the point where it starts breaks down, so that as the body repairs it you get more and stronger muscle.

How do you become stronger within yourself? By going through tough times, learning, and growing in your understanding and ability to respond to challenges.

Look at every Superhero out there today. They've all gone through their trials. Would Batman be who he is if his parents hadn't been killed? Spiderman lost his uncle. Superman's entire world was destroyed. That's what set them on the path to further ups and downs and to whom they are today. It's the same with you: the grand total of all your experiences make you who you are.

So start honoring your life – all of it. Realize that all of what you've gone through is simply a part of your story. And what's so cool is that *you* get to write your story as it goes along. Right here in the present, the pen is on the paper, and you get to dictate what it writes. When things are tough, are you going to roll up in a ball and let life win? Or are you going to use the challenges you're facing as a turning point, an excuse to reframe things, take total ownership, and use your phenomenal courage, intelligence, and willpower to creating something great?

That's what Soul-Centered Leaders do. They embrace themselves fully. They don't run and hide from their pasts or their shadow aspects—they don't pretend that the past never happened or that their shadow doesn't exist. They know it's just one part of their story.

Appreciate your Gifts

Remember earlier I talked about how everything is really about your relationship with yourself? How you perceive yourself and your own abilities goes a long way towards shaping what you do with yourself in life.

For example, did you know that dyslexia is more common among entrepreneurs?[3] Why would that be? At first thought dyslexia is a problem anyone would be better without, but if you reframe it you can understand how it has actually served many entrepreneurs. The challenges of dyslexia often force dyslexics to learn resilience early on, such as how to deal with people, communicate a vision, and to push through challenges. In fact, it turns out that many leaders have suffered hardships in early in life, which can lead to them learning the skills needed to overcome difficult situations and motivate themselves and others.[4]

You can start to realize that when "bad" things happen, it's just

---

[3] http://www.nytimes.com/2007/12/05/business/worldbusiness/05iht-dyslexia.4.8602036.html?_r=0

[4] https://www.andrews.edu/services/jacl/current_issue/hardship-and-leadership-is-there-a-connection-.html

the natural process of a Hero going through their growth and strengthening. That's what the idea of the hero's Journey helps you with; unconditional self-love and self-acceptance. It's a way to understand challenges as progress on the road to overcoming the shadow and achieving victory. It's another way to build your self-esteem and understand how awesome you are.

You *are* amazing. You're a Hero who's been trying to convince yourself you aren't one.

This is all part of your story. What's going to happen next?

That's up to you. The pen is in your hand. Always remember, you can write your own story.

In Real Life

When you catch yourself negatively judging something in your past, think instead about how that particular challenge, event or relationship contributed to your power now. How would things have been different if that difficulty had never been a part of your life?

When you recognize a strength in yourself, quickly trace it back to a situation you've been through. This is another way of reinforcing how challenges become learning experiences and skill builders.

When you see other people down on themselves about something, can you help them see how it's part of their own hero's journey?

Look at different aspects of your life. Play with the idea of the hero's journey, seeing how that template has played out in your relationships, your career, your business and so on.

Go to the exercises to write your own Hero's Journey.

Access the exercises through the membership site at http://tiny.cc/scl-member

Dark Night of the Soul

There may be a few times in your life when things look absolutely bleak. Like there's no way out. Deaths, divorces, lawsuits, sicknesses, breakups, bankruptcies . . . Sometimes you can't even identify a particular reason—it just feels as if life has been sucked dry of its joy and nothing makes sense anymore. You feel alone, unable to connect with others. You lose all sense of purpose, and wonder, "What's the point of it all?"

This is the despair stage in the Heroes Journey chapter. There's a spiritual term to describe a period like this in your life: the "dark night of the soul." If you're going through this kind of tough time, this chapter is for you. Think of this as your "break glass in case of emergency" chapter. Even though it references skills taught later in the book, I placed it here because it's such a powerful, challenging stage in the hero's journey. Understanding the "dark night of the soul" in this way can help you move through it—and use it to expand yourself and deepen your experience of life. The chapter can also be used to support others who are in the despair phase.

Life's Roller Coaster

Personally, I've gone through some real low lows in my life. Times where I didn't know if I was going to make it, where part of me just wanted to give up.

There's the time I moved to Singapore to run sales for an international software company, and within two months all five of the people in my sales department quit within three weeks of each other-because of my arrogance. There I was in a foreign country, supposedly the hot-shot American sales superstar, and I lost the whole team. I was failing in a big way.

Another time, I was pretty sure that the company I founded and grew wouldn't make payroll for the next thirty days. This was the company I had built up from nothing. I had my whole identity attached to it, and it was going to fail. I couldn't sleep. I couldn't think of anything else. Just what would happen if I lost it all?

I've already told you about the time my business partner, who was also my COO, assaulted me, causing me to file a restraining order against him and terminate him (which I talk about in My Story). This was right while my divorce was in full swing. At the time, I felt like my world was collapsing in around me. It was an effort to get out of bed in the morning; which sometimes didn't even happen.

There are people who go thorough much worse than this, I know; I only bring up these dark times from my own life to let you know that I'm certainly not perfect, and that we all have these tests in our lives.

The fact is, the Universe is preparing you for something great, though it sure doesn't feel like it during these times.

The dark night of the soul can be thought of as preparation on the soul-level. Just like any other dark night, morning will arrive, and it will be magnificent. If you can recognize this and stick with the challenges, see them through, you will come out of it with a new sense of enlightenment.

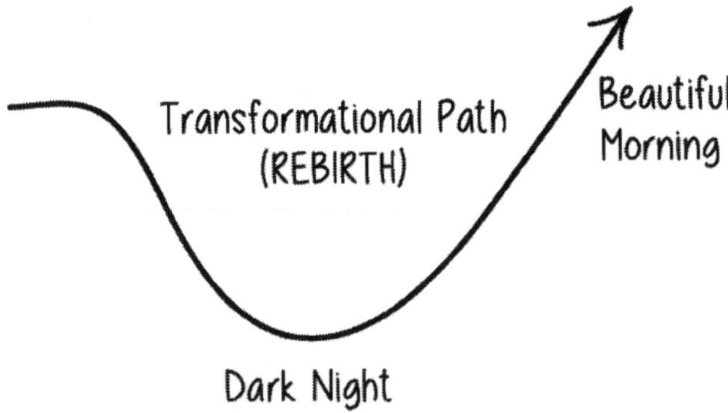

But you don't just have to weather the storm in a passive state of mind. The good news is that there are many things you can do to pass through this phase more quickly while still honoring it and supporting yourself.

Your Road Map Home

Here are some things you can do to bring yourself through it. Follow each point. They're all important, so don't let your ego talk you out of any of them.

- **Acknowledgement** - First, admit that you're going through a tough time. Quit trying to ignore it, hoping it will go away. Doing so will only increase your anxiety anyway and increase the energy you're expending trying to resist it. Instead acknowledge it. That lets the pressure boil off and allow you to really move into a supporting place for yourself. Let it be okay that you're feeling down. Remember what you learned in Letting Go chapter: when you accept your feelings, you will move through them much faster.

- **Self-Care** - This is *not* a time for you to isolate yourself with alcohol or drugs. Up your health game. Quit drinking for a while, and stay away from drugs of all sorts if at all possible (the exception, of course, being under doctor's orders—but *do* let your doc know what you're going through.) You're probably going to want to binge eat as well – DON'T DO THAT. Instead, eat healthy. Exercise. Do yoga. Walk outside. I know you won't want to. Do it anyway.

- **Focus on Yourself** - Look at what's going on in your life right now. As much as possible, take anything off the schedule that isn't supportive or helping you get through the current crisis. See what other obligations you can get out of. If that work party isn't what you feel you need at the moment, gracefully get out of it. Take any coffee, lunch, and networking get-togethers off your schedule if they aren't going to give you a lift. Focus on the critical things; everything else can wait. Every-day review your to-do list and purge it of unnecessary items. If you have free time see the above point; go and exercise, get a massage, nurture yourself.

- **Ask the Experts** - Get professional help – especially if you are going through a depression,[5] and absolutely if you are seriously contemplating suicide.[6] You may not want to. You may really resist it with a kind of stoicism and can-do attitude that may serve you in other aspects of life. But just go and have one conversation with a professional about it. You owe that much to yourself. Take a chance on getting some help in healing yourself. If no one else is available, contact me.

- **Ask for and accept help** - Call up a good friend. Ask them if they wouldn't mind just listening. Then tell them what you're going through. Admit your feelings. Yes, I know it's hard – you want to do this all on your own. Drop that right now. This is a huge growth opportunity to let someone else in right now and simply *receive*. The intention here is to get through this dark night as soon as possible, without ignoring or dismissing it. To that end, open yourself to every supportive tool you can use. The fact is, too, that your friends would very likely love to help you. Wouldn't you help them if they were going through the same thing?

  On that note, if someone calls *you* when they're in this heavy state of mind, remember that you're not there to give advice, tell them what you think, or anything like that. They just need you to listen. This may be uncomfortable; you'll probably want to say something that you think will help them. You might even feel it's important to tell them that they're wrong, things aren't that bad, or whatever. They don't need that. They just need you to be with them. Just listen and love them.

- **Work your Processes** – After a few days of rest, which can be beneficial, stop laying on the couch and binge watching TV shows. Do things that will uplift you. Read something uplifting. Open yourself to new ideas. Many of the exercises in this book will go a long way toward helping you through this. Keep in mind this is part of your personal Hero's Journey.

---

5 http://www.webmd.com/depression/guide/detecting-depression

6 http://www.suicide.org/suicide-hotlines.html

- **Remember it has an end** - Repeat this mantra "...and this too shall pass." It reminds you that everything is temporary, including whatever you're going through right now.
- **You're a risk taker** - People who go for it in life have great ups – with some downs. It's a tough part of life, but it is also one that in many cases teaches some of life's most valuable lessons. And it's these times that help mold your character, resilience, and strength. The dark night of the soul is part of the human experience.

So above all, remember. Give yourself a break. Be at peace with going through this. Don't judge it, just let it be. This is not a sign of weakness—it's a sign of evolution and personal development. You will come out of it stronger. You're still awesome, and better things are on the horizon.

Think about this point too: anyone can be a leader when things are going well. It's the individuals who rise up and stick with it when things are tough who are Soul-Centered Leaders.

There aren't any additional sections in this chapter. If you're in a time of need, simply reread the chapter and follow the road map above. Practice your self-compassion. You're worth it...and you deserve it.

15. Forgiveness

Do you recall in the chapter My Story where I told you about how my business partner assaulted me in my own office?

I owned the majority of the company, and after our exchange I fired him and filed a restraining order and a lawsuit. We both had a lot of anger against one another, and the lawsuit turned ugly very quickly.

Then, he started a competing company, hired one of my senior technical people away from me, and started stealing my clients.

I don't think I'd ever felt so much anger against another person before. I let it dominate my life. I hated him with every fiber of my being. I carried the anger around with me all the time; when I heard his name I got tense. I had bad dreams about him. It was everywhere. You know the state you get in where you can basically feel the emotions as if you're literally carrying them around inside you? That's how heavy and consuming my anger was.

But there was a major silver lining. All this was going on around the time I started my Master's Degree in Spiritual Psychology at the University of Santa Monica. This turned out great, because I was learning techniques at USM that I could apply to the challenges I was dealing with involving this guy, the lawsuit, and all these ego-based emotions.

One of the major things we were learning about in class was forgiveness. Typically following a lecture, we break up into small groups to practice what we just learned. One day I found myself sitting across from a woman, a fellow student, who was counseling me through a forgiveness exercise.

She opened our discussion with, "Who are you upset with?"

I answered with a classic denial. "Ah, no one, really. I'm pretty good with everyone."

She was smarter than that. "No, really, who are you upset with?"

I decided to open up. After all, I was going through the program for a reason . . . "Okay, okay . . . Right now I really hate my old business partner."

"That's a great start. So why are you so upset with him?"

I laid it all out for her. "Well, we got into a big disagreement about ownership of the company and he hit me in the middle of my office. So I kicked him out of the company. Now we're in the middle of a really nasty lawsuit. On top of that, he started a competitor. He's stealing away my people and taking my customers. Can you believe that?" Just talking about it had gotten me riled up, and I let loose with, "Ahhhh! What an asshole!"

My fellow student remained calm, and I could sense her compassion. She was good at this. "Got it," she said. "I can really hear from you that this is causing you upset. But let me ask you this: How is his world different with you hating him?"

I was confused. "I'm not sure what you're asking."

"Well," she explained, "You spend your time and energy resenting this guy. But does it affect his day-to-day life whether you're upset with him or not?"

What she was saying suddenly hit me. My resentment and hatred weren't affecting him at all. It was only generating negativity in my own life. My upset was all about me, not him. It had never occurred to me to look at it like that, but when I did, the craziness of that way of doing things was clear. What a waste of energy!

I sat there in a daze while this sunk in. She took advantage of my silence to say, "Let's look at it a different way for a second. If you were in his situation—granted you might not have hit someone—but if you were kicked out of a company that you helped build, and if you felt angry as hell, what would you do?"

I knew right away, but I didn't like to see it in myself. I decided to be honest. "I would start a competitor and steal away people and clients."

"So maybe you can have a little bit of compassion for him? See things from his side, just a tiny bit?"

I laughed. "Yes, I believe I can."

"Forgiveness really isn't for or about the other person. It's for you. Can you forgive your business partner?"

I took a deep breath.

"Yes, I forgive my business partner."

I know it may sound unbelievable, but in that moment, I really felt like a weight had lifted off my shoulders. I took all that negativity and resentment that I had been weighing myself down with, and

I released it. Just like that it was gone.

People often ask me, is it really that easy?

It can be. While sometimes it takes time, I've witnessed, both in myself and others, magical releases of a huge issue in a single moment.

Getting Rid of Baggage

There is truth underlying the metaphor of "a weight being lifted" from us when we let go of negativity, resentment, worry and so on. Carrying around these emotions interferes with our ability to engage in other, more productive activities. When we let them go, we can engage with far less distraction and negative mental pressure. As a Soul-Centered Leader, you need this. You need your energy freed up, because creation and leadership—the good stuff—need focus and fuel. They need positive mental pressure.

> ***When you are upset with yourself, another person, or a situation, the only result of that is negativity within your own self.***

As a leader, people are going to take their cue from you. They'll follow how *you* do things. And if you act that with resentment and hatred, you're not going to create a very conscious environment. The more you hold onto these judgments around others, the less you are connected to your soul. Focus your energy on creativity, not on holding grudges.

Need more convincing? Studies[7] have linked forgiveness to better health and better performance.

Keep in mind that everybody – *everybody* – is doing what they, on some level, think is right at any particular point in time, given the information they have on hand. It's your job to accept that they made the decision they did, that it's not your job to judge, and then to let it go.

---

[7] http://journals.sagepub.com/doi/abs/10.1177/1948550614564222

I have countless examples of times when I moved from judgment to forgiveness, and this resulted in a transformed relationships and new opportunities. Nowadays when I find myself judging someone, I make it a point to move into a compassionate place and often engage the individual from that state of being.

For example, I was once mentoring a young woman who had tremendous potential, but she had been brought up in a difficult environment. There was a position available at a high-profile organization, and I knew it would be a good fit for her. I also happened to know people there and could set up and interview. So I told her about it.

I was a little taken aback when she said, "That's a stupid place to work. I would never want to work there."

At first I went into judgment, thinking to myself: *She doesn't even know anything about the place. It's a great opportunity for her, and I'm calling in a favor. Why is she being so difficult?*

For a minute I was angry—then I caught myself and went into forgiveness. In doing so I freed up the energy that would've otherwise been wasted in anger. Without that distraction it was easier to check inside myself; my intuition told me there was more to what was going on with her than it appeared at first. I decided to meet her with compassion.

I continued talking with her, asking her, in different ways, why she didn't even want to go for the interview. After about the fifth different way of asking her, all with compassion and patience, she finally admitted, "It's something I've never done before. I'm scared of not doing a good job and letting you down."

As leaders, when you see others making excuses, putting things off, being critical, and not giving 100%, realize that's normally because they have *fear of failure*. This was certainly the case with this young woman, and she was about to throw away a good opportunity because of her fear. And if I hadn't checked my own anger, I would have helped her throw it away.

Just as you are learning to build your self-worth and self-esteem, you can support others in doing the same. Especially as a Soul-Centered Leader.

Soul-Centered Leaders meet people's fears with compassion, and then they help them recognize their self-worth and regain their self-esteem.

It's Their Own Path

I had another friend, another business owner, who all of a sudden was just flat out rude to me over and over out of the blue. I didn't understand why. Many of our friends were also experiencing the same thing with her, so I knew it wasn't something I had done. But I was concerned, so I looked into what was happening in her life.

It turned out that her daughter had become involved with drugs. My friend was running around at all hours of the night trying to keep her daughter alive. On top of this the situation was putting strain on her marriage.

It would have been so easy for me to judge her for her rudeness and leave it at that. (I know I have done things like this in my life before, without realizing it, and before I learned these tools.) But the fact is she was incredibly overwhelmed. She needed my support—not my judgment—but she wasn't asking for it. Once her other friends and I found out what was going on we were able to provide support. If we had just passed judgment on her, none of us would've truly felt better.

Remember that when people are rude to you, it's a projection of some aspect of their own relationship with themselves. I've been working on this material for so long that when someone comes to me upset, instead of meeting that with more of the same I tell myself, "There's something going on in their inner world that is causing this. It isn't me. I wonder what it could be?" And I meet them with compassion.

By the same token, when I catch myself getting triggered and reactionary, I look at what's going on in my own life. More than once I've snapped at someone then realized I was putting myself under a lot more pressure than I needed to. When this happens, I prescribe some time off and meditation for myself, and I work on some of the exercises that you're learning in this book.

Take Ownership and Act

Taking the first step in a troubled relationship can be life-changing as well. Sometimes it even seems as if the universe rewards us when that happens.

During my software days, both my firm and a competitor were doing work for a large client. This was a complex, multi-million dollar project that spanned over a year. There were a lot of grey areas that either our people or theirs could work on – and gain revenue from. In addition, there was some finger pointing over things that didn't turn out just right. My competitor and I had some tense conversations, sometimes just between us, but other times in front of our teams and sometimes even the client.

After the project was completed, I saw him at a trade show, so I and walked over to talk with him. It was the first time we had ever met face to face. I introduced myself and said, "Dave, I know it was a challenging project. I just want to say that my team said your people were extremely good technically and a pleasure to work with. I know we had some differences, but I also want you to know that I find you a person of very high integrity, and I have a lot of respect for you." He looked at me for a second then broke into a smile, invited me for a drink, and we ended up becoming fast friends and collaborators for the next few years.

I find that a specific, heartfelt complement, while looking the person softly in the eyes, can transform almost any relationship. But you can't do this if you're still holding on to anger and petty grudges, or if you carry beliefs about, for example, how you have to be a lone wolf in order to succeed.

The Type of Leader People Follow

When you hold something against someone, it doesn't just suck up energy in you. When it leaks out and someone hears you judging another person, one of two things happen: 1) A separation is created, because the person overhearing you doesn't want to be the next one to feel your wrath, or 2) they pick up the same behavior. When you show up judgmental and critical, you are implicitly giving them permission to be the same way. If you're their boss, they may even join in with your anger at the other person in order to get on your good side—maybe it's safer for them that way.

Think about all the people against whom you hold anger, a grudge or just any bad feeling right now. If you could wave a magic wand and let all the negative emotion go away, what would your life be like? Would you have more space for optimism, strategy, leadership?

You bet you would.

Forgiveness of another person is the second-best way to release negativity and free up your energy. The next chapter will teach you the number one way. But first, do the exercises below. Free that space up, move forward, and lead.

In Real Life

Do you catch yourself judging others and then talking about them negatively to other people? Stop that now! You are spreading negativity and lessening your effectiveness as a leader.

When you catch yourself in upset with someone, set a clear intention to let it go. Move past what's "right" and "wrong." Consider taking the first step in meeting with this person. Find something positive about them, and let them know you appreciate that quality.

When you get upset with someone, play a game. Think of all the reasons they might have done what they have done. Think up both heavy reasons (maybe their spouse just left them, maybe they got abused as a child), and light ones (maybe they really have to go to the bathroom!) It reminds you that you don't know what's behind their actions, and this helps you generate compassion for them.

When you're upset with someone, take 100% ownership for your part in the disagreement, even if it's a small part. It sets a great example for your people and will give the other person an opening to do the same (but remember to be unattached to the outcome regardless of whether they take ownership or not; that part is not in your control.)

Another real-time forgiveness practice is to breath out the upset. Feel the tension in your body, breath in, and as you breathe out, feel the negativity leave with your exhalation.

Access the exercises through the membership site at http://tiny.cc/scl-member

16. Self-Forgiveness and Compassion

I may have been able to forgive my business partner and my ex-wife, but I was still judging myself. My inner dialog was unforgiving:

You're so stupid for getting into business with that guy!

You wasted so much time by marrying that woman, and now of course it's ending in divorce. You should have known better.

You're so stupid, Michael...Really, quit making so many mistakes

I was lacking any sort of love or compassion for myself. Instead I was trapped in a vicious circle of blame and self-recrimination that was making it all but impossible to heal and move forward with my life. I had yet to learn the most powerful action you can take to heal your relationship with yourself: Self-Forgiveness.

In my Master's program, self-forgiveness was the keynote skill. The university waited until we were already a year through the course before even introducing it to us. Once they did, we worked on mastering it for the entire second year.

In fact, all of us are still working on it. Self-forgiveness is a life-long journey. It can feel counterintuitive at first because it requires that you accept and show compassion to sides of yourself and actions you've taken that you might rather forget. But because self-forgiveness is so fundamental to our well-being and happiness, I encourage you to stick with it. Reread the relevant chapters and continue going through the exercises until it becomes a habit. Or better yet, join and get active in the Soul-Centered Leadership community, where I'll have many opportunities for you to grow in your own personal evolution. You'll be able to play with these ideas, experiment with them, and see how well you can incorporate them into your life.

It's well worth the effort.

Give Yourself some Grace

We've already talked about how judging you as "wrong" or "bad" isn't a healthy place to be. By forgiving yourself and accepting that you're not perfect, you return to a state of love, compassion, and acceptance for yourself. Self-forgiveness lets you off the hook, gives you a break, and boosts your self-esteem.

The most important change you can ever make is to come into a more loving and compassionate relationship with yourself. The best strategy for doing this is learning self-forgiveness.

You're always going to do things that aren't perfect. It's part of your humanness. To forgive yourself, simply figure out what judgments you're holding against yourself – and let them go.

Of course, this can be easier said than done.

When it comes to forgiving yourself for doing something wrong—or at least something you perceive as wrong—you don't need or want to forgive yourself for the action itself. You simply want to forgive yourself for the judgment you've been making about yourself related to that action.

Let's stay with this idea for a minute. When you forgive yourself, you can still accept that you did do something you may wish you hadn't, something you might choose to handle differently now. The action isn't something you can change; you can only accept that it's what you did at the time. What you can change is whether or not you continue to judge yourself for taking it.

It's our judgment of the action, and of ourselves for taking it, that we want to release.

Forgiveness is letting go. It's showing compassion to the part of you that made the decision, telling it that it's okay, regardless of any potential consequences. It was doing what it thought was right at the time.

You're Always Doing the Best You Can

As an example, take me partnering up with my ex-business partner. When I started the company I had fear about doing it alone, so I end up giving this guy—someone I didn't know that well—equity in the business. Of course, looking back, I can see this was not the best decision. But it's easy to judge it that way now. And if I do I'm judging myself from back then. From the perspective of everything that's happened since then, it's easy to judge him and call him stupid.

But the truth is that the Michael back then was doing the absolute best he could. He didn't have a crystal ball. In fact, he was doing an amazing thing: he was starting a company from scratch and experiencing some great success. Sure, he wasn't perfect. He didn't always make the most astute decisions—certainly not from the business school point of view. But the truth is he was doing something he had never done before, something most people only dream of yet never even try, much less become successful at. That Michael took on a great deal of risk and stress, as well as a business partner who didn't work out for the long term.

I am not forgiving the fact that I took on that business partner. I am accepting it, and myself, for doing it. What I forgive is this:

I forgive the fact that I have been judging myself for bringing him on. I release the judgment around that and come into peace and compassion for myself.

Notice in the above that two things are happening: Not only am I forgiving myself, I am also reminding myself of the conditions surrounding why I took the actions I did. I am reframing how I look at the situation, and in using the phrase "the truth is" I highlight the courageous, strong actions I did take back then but which I have been ignoring in favor of judgment and self-recrimination.

Let's say you go through a divorce and feel a lot of bitterness towards yourself for getting married in the first place. When you go to release that, you aren't forgiving yourself for getting married, nor for getting the divorce. At the time of both events you made what you thought was the right move given the information that was available. Besides, even if you can't see your way clear to understanding or reframing why you made whatever "mistake" you made in the past, the action itself is not the important thing. That's done. It is, after all, in the past. What's in the present—the only thing you can act upon—is the judgment you hold against yourself.

In a way, trying to forgive yourself for your actions is like trying to erase the past. We can't do this, and there's no point in trying. What's more, when we look back at whom we were then, and why we made the decisions we did, we are rewarded with powerful insights into who we can become. We see how we allowed our energy to get dammed up behind judgments and regrets, and we empower ourselves to release that energy and use it to become the creative powerhouses we are.

It's all part of our hero's journey.

Remember the above chapter on judging? Think of it in those terms: You aren't judging the divorce. The divorce wasn't wrong. The only truth is that it is. This is why everything becomes about acceptance, and then about the releasing of judgments through forgiveness.

So you release the judgment that the divorce was wrong. You come into acceptance of everything that happened. You cut yourself slack for not automatically being perfect all the time. You accept and love your humanness.

We can be so hard on ourselves! Do you experience a constant negative chatter in your mind? The type that reminds you of everything you haven't done perfectly? Self-forgiveness is the antidote to that voice. Practice it enough and the chatter doesn't just go away; the voice changes into one of positivity and support.

Keep in mind that anyone, including and especially you, is always doing their best, making whatever choices seem right at any given point in time. You forget that when you start judging yourself.

The Key to Freedom

The Freedom to Choose Project gave me the most profound experiences of my life. Participants in the Freedom to Choose Foundation go into maximum security prisons and teach the inmates love and forgiveness. Yes, that's right: they teach love and forgiveness to murderers, armed robbers, and gang members. What's more, the inmates are spectacular students.

Its name references a Viktor Frankl quote:

> "Everything can be taken from a man but one thing: the last of the human freedoms—to choose one's attitude in any given set of circumstances, to choose one's own way."
>
> **— Viktor E. Frankl, Man's Search for Meaning**

When we teach the inmates self-forgiveness, we aren't teaching them to, for example, forgive themselves for murdering someone. Instead, we teach them to come into acceptance with what they've done, to remember that at any given time they are doing the absolute best they can, given what they know and the circumstances in which they find themselves. What they can do is let go of the judgments they've made around that and bring a little bit more kindness and compassion to themselves and into their lives.

To clarify: we don't say that murdering someone or committing a crime is right or wrong. We stay out of that equation altogether; that's not what we're there for. What we do teach is that there's no use holding on to that negativity. It's time to move on. We also teach the inmates that they—and all of us—are responsible for their actions. Coming into self-forgiveness helps them to accept this responsibility and learn about healthier choices for action.

In my work with inmates I witnessed some of them letting go of so much go in a single instant that it changed their lives. One woman said that during this process she felt valued for the first time in her life. Others have shared that they let go of judgments that had been paralyzing them from ever moving forward in their lives.

Outside of the prison I've worked with many others using the same techniques. One powerful business woman I know was incredibly hard on herself despite being highly driven and successful. Yet no matter how much money she made, she never experienced the smallest hint of satisfaction. Her work was taking an enormous toll on her health.

I worked with her on following that hard-driving voice within her back to its source. This was the voice that was always telling her she wasn't good enough, that she had to do more, more, more. We followed that voice through her past until she remembered that when she was a small child she was beaten by her parents when she didn't do her chores—and in fact even sometimes when she did. While they were physically abusing her, they would also berate her and tell her how she wasn't doing enough.

Just to survive, that little girl inside of her made an agreement that in order to be safe, she always had to try to do more. She had set herself up for a battle that, in the present, she could never win. And as illogical as it sounds, some part of her judged that little girl for not doing enough, and for bringing the abuse upon herself.

When we uncovered this, she worked on forgiving the little girl inside of her, letting her know that she hadn't ever done anything wrong. The truth was that she was perfect and lovable just the way she was. This became a turning point in her life.

And this is just one of many powerful examples of how when you're locked in an invisible, self-created, subconscious prison, self-compassion can be the key to freedom.

Self-Forgiveness Statements

Creating a self-forgiveness statement will help you focus and clarify your particular issue. The key to remember when creating it is to forgive, then anchor in the truth. Self-forgiveness statements typically start out like:

"I forgive myself for judging myself as . . ."

"I forgive myself for buying into the misbelief that ..."

Following this, and to anchor your statement in the affirmative, state the truth:

"The truth is . . ."

Here are examples of affirmations for someone who's just been through a divorce:

"I forgive myself for judging myself as stupid for marrying her. I forgive myself for buying into the misbelief that I should have known better. The truth is that I took a risk, and at that time I really thought it would work out. The truth is that I learned so much about myself and relationships in general that I would probably have never learned without undergoing the experience."

Here's one that was appropriate for my situation with my former business partner. Note again that I am not forgiving myself for getting into business with him. I am forgiving myself for my judgments.

"I forgive myself for judging myself to be a bad business person. I forgive myself for buying into the misbelief that I should have done things differently. The truth is that I created a great company, and that I learned so much about business, partnerships, and the legal system. Even though it ended up in a lawsuit, he helped me build the company in the early days. There was no way for me to know it would end up like this, and who knows if I would have been successful making other decisions anyway?"

The process works in smaller areas in life, too, of course. Let's say you're a leader who lost your temper when one of your people didn't finish a task on time. Sure, you're upset with them, but you're more frustrated with yourself, because you're usually fair and even-tempered. As part of working out what went wrong and healing the relationship with your employee, you might start with:

"I forgive myself for judging myself an idiot for losing my temper with Bob in front of the sales team. I forgive myself for buying into the misbelief that I must always be in control of my emotions and can never slip up and have an outburst. The truth is, I'm human too, and sometimes my frustration can get the better of me. The truth is I'm generally a kind, fair and well-meaning person."

Can you see how this process will put you in a better state of mind to address your relationship with your employee? It will very likely incline you to apologize, admit that you lost your temper, and then move on—with your energy freed up to address the practical issues under discussion when you initially lost your temper.

If you lost a big sale and are down on yourself because people were counting on you, it may be "I forgive myself for judging myself as a failure. The truth is that I'm very successful, and that I gave it my all."

If you plain made a mistake that people saw and you're embarrassed about, try "I forgive myself for judging myself as stupid. The truth is that I sometimes do make mistakes...yet I'm still intelligent and driven, and worthy as a human being. The truth is in fact that I do a heck of a lot more right than I get wrong!"

I've worked the self-forgiveness process on myself over and over and over. I'm at the place now where if I catch myself judging myself in real-time, I can do a quick release and self-forgiveness statement right then and there. For example, if I take the wrong exit on the highway and it looks like I'll be late, my internal chatter might say, "Mike, that was stupid! Why did you turn there?"

If that happens, I am usually aware of it, and I'll say something like, "I forgive myself for judging myself as stupid. It's okay that I made a wrong turn. The truth is I'm still a worthy person."

That might seem like a lot for a simple wrong turn! But it works. It does the trick, and keeps me from getting bogged down in useless mental chatter.

Leading from the Authentic Self

How does this relate to the idea of Soul-Centered Leadership?

As a leader—and of course as a human being—you need to get rid of the baggage that's keeping you from being truly conscious, connected, and evolved. Your thinking and behavior are distorted by your insecurities, which in turn arise from judgments you have against yourself.

How can you ask others to follow you when you don't even trust or believe in yourself?

Follow this process through. When a situation triggers you, instead of reacting, take ownership of how you show up. Identify all the projections, identities, judgments, self-limiting beliefs, and anything else that's holding you back. And then let them go.

Following up with self-forgiveness and acknowledging the truth of who you are anchors the process. This is the ultimate exercise in accepting yourself, and it opens you up to be able to intimately connect with others. Your natural reserves of strength, creativity, wonder, compassion and more can bubble up from your Authentic Self without encountering so much interference along the way. You become so secure in yourself that people naturally follow you because they feed off of your courage and confidence.

Can you see how this process creates powerful leaders?

The next time something doesn't work out as expected, instead of getting down on you and going into a depression or blaming someone else, take a minute to release any judgments and address the issue. When you interact with others who are being hard on themselves, you can use these tools to coach them into a better place.

As we said above, if you have that little voice in the back of your mind always chirping negativity at you, you can turn it into a cheerleader instead. Just keep practicing self-forgiveness and instead of judging you, it will bring encouragement. What would you, as a leader, look like with that kind of confidence and connection to yourself and others?

In Real Life

When you hear the little critical voice start chattering your head, just listen to it without judgment. Don't react, and certainly don't swallow everything it tells you! Just listen, and then send it compassion.

While I know this may sound like a strange and counterintuitive thing to do, it's really a form of self-acceptance. With practice it becomes easy and even natural. I've been working on this for years now, and I can very often forgive myself in real-time, even for simple things like dropping something on the ground. Whereas before I might have automatically called myself dumb, I now catch the self-judgment and forgive it right then and there.

Keep in mind that you are always doing the best you can. When you feel uncomfortable or anxious, chuckle to yourself and remember that this is part of your humanness.

If you catch yourself judging your past, remember that it's all part of your Hero's Journey. Take a moment to consider how it's shaped your experiences today, and how in recognizing this you can move forward with resilience and courage.

Actually go so far as to expect yourself and your team to make mistakes. They will happen. It's not your job to be perfect, but it is your job to keep moving forward, take risks, clean up the messes you do make and joyfully accept your successes.

Keep an eye out for others who are judging themselves. This can take them into a downward spiral. Sit down, talk with and really listen to them. Then build them back up; tell them all the great things you see in them. Be specific. Look them in the eye. Send them love and compassion.

When you need courage to do something big, whether it's a phone call, presentation, or interview, give yourself a break. Remind yourself that it may or may not work out, that you are just going to be you, and the rest will take care of itself. No matter what happens, you'll be alright.

Follow the exercises in the chapter to work a process where you identify and release judgments against yourself.

Access the exercises through the membership site at http://tiny.cc/scl-member

17. Intuition

You have within you a secret weapon, but you're only using a tiny, tiny piece of it. It's your intuition. You might know it as your "gut feeling" or your "instinct." What it really is, is an inner knowing tied to the universe and your higher power.

When you follow your intuition rather than chase ego-based goals, the universe gives more than you ever imagined.

Your intuition is always guiding you to the highest-level action available to you. It's a very real thing, and getting in touch with it - and even more so trusting it - can be a game changer. You already use it, but now it's time to develop it further and learn to trust it. Here's a great exercise to get started:

Write down the three greatest things that have ever happened to you. Focus on business, but it could include something in your personal life. These could include sales you've achieved, a product or innovation you've come up with, meeting a partner / spouse...Once you've done this, reflect on each situation.

When you look deeper into each one, did something happen that statically never should have happened in order to make that a reality? Is it like something was invisibly helping you? Maybe you'd been cold-calling prospects for years, but when it came to that monster sale, it was the result of meeting someone in a taxi line. Or it could be that you'd been on a thousand dates, and just as you gave up on finding a partner you end up sitting next to the most perfect person on a plane, and six months later you're married.

Look at the top three on your list. See how they've moved your life forward. What if you had experiences like these all the time?

That's what we are opening up for you here. Once you let go of what you should do, along with all the attachments around it, and have an intention to create, your higher power rewards you. What will come into your life is astounding. Keep in mind that this happens far more easily and often once you've cleared the path to your

Authentic Self. There's so much less static for the messages to get through.

This can be called co-creation, because at this state you are so dialed into your higher power that both of you are part of the construction. Your higher power shows you the path, and you take it. Co-creation.

Think of intuition as your direct line to the universe. The universe has these great ideas for you. It offers them up, and if you're tuned in, if you're mindful, present and aware of what's going on inside you, you'll notice and take the new ideas to heart. If you're not paying attention to your intuition, you're going to miss the opportunities.

All the tools you've been learning in this book—overcoming self-limiting beliefs, forgiveness, self-forgiveness, mindfulness, etc.—all put you in a more intuitive place. You can feel and see the flow of life much more clearly when working your process and using these skills.

On the other hand, if you're too focused on ego-based goals and have your blinders on because you're driving yourself relentlessly towards a single outcome, you won't see any of the paths along the way that just might lead to greater, and maybe even faster, acts of creation.

Accidentally Acquiring a Company

Many people have incredible stories about how intuition has played a seemingly miraculous role in their life. Here's one of mine:

At one point when I was CEO of two rapidly growing software companies, I noticed that I was so busy that I wasn't getting my most important priorities done. In order to focus, I decided I had to stop all non-essential tasks, such as networking and casual calls. Then one day an old colleague and I were talking on the phone about an unrelated matter, and she suggested I talk with her boss, whom she liked. He ran the division of a CPA firm that was in the same business as we were. She didn't really have a reason for making the suggestion; she just for some reason thought that it would be a good contact for me to make. Unfortunately it was exactly the kind of activity I had vowed not to do in order to maintain my focus on what I considered to be my priorities.

A few days later she sent the e-mail with his contact information, and I filed it away, figuring I would just blow it off. The only problem was that I had a small, nagging feeling that I should call this guy. So after a few days I gave in and called him. We had a pleasant, forty-five minute conversation without any real agenda, action items, or outcome.

"Oh well," I thought, and then didn't think much more about it after that.

A few months later, our industry held a conference. As I received the e-mail invite, for some unknown reason, this guy came to mind. I dropped him a note about it coming up in two weeks and asked if he was going. He quickly replied by email, saying he didn't know about it, but yes, he was going to find a way to get there even though it was last minute.

At the conference, I was on my way out to dinner with a few other people. Even though there were literally hundreds of people there, I bumped into a guy, looked at his name tag, and realized it was the same CPA I'd invited. I asked if he would join us for dinner. We had a great dinner and went out on the town, as of course you sometimes you do at conferences. He asked a lot of questions about me and our company and I was very forthcoming and transparent. It turned out he ran a few business units of the CPA firm and he didn't have a lot of experience in our industry.

We spent some more time together during the conference and parted at the end with a good relationship and mutual trust and respect.

A few weeks later I got a message asking me to call him. So I did.

He wanted to sell me his division. For him, it was a distraction to the main business of the rest of the CPA firm. I asked him the price; he said I would only have to pay a nominal fee upfront, and then I could just pay him a small percentage of the revenue from the customer base. I could bring over any of the staff I wanted.

I took him up on his offer, and it turned out to double my company's revenue overnight. It was hugely profitable. I brought on skilled staff, and had to pay almost nothing for it. And it all came from following my intuition. Look at how many things almost didn't happen, though each was necessary for the final result:

I almost didn't call the guy.

I almost didn't invite him to the conference, and he ended up coming at the last minute.

I almost didn't bump into him on the way out to dinner in the middle of a huge conference.

And then there I was, with double the company, for almost no cost.

Your Connection to More

Intuition, your gut-feeling, inner knowing; they're all referring to the same phenomena. They're how your higher power talks to you, your hotline to the divine. All you just have to do is listen for it.

There are steps to make these downloads more accessible. First set the intention to be open to receiving inner guidance. You can ask anytime: before a meditation, before going to sleep, before going into a meeting, and so on. Then simply open up, be quiet and listen. You may not receive messages like bolts out of the blue. It might not even happen immediately, but by setting the intention and giving it the space to play out, you are honoring that voice inside you—and it will make itself heard.

A word of warning: The ego can be good at masquerading as the intuition. What that means is that sometimes you get a message that you think is your inner guidance, but really it's your ego that's fighting for its life and wants to be back in control.

It's your job to figure out the difference.

Messages from the ego will sound like: I need to control. . . I have fear about . . .What will happen if . . . ?

They will often be accompanied by stress or anxiety. They may also involve criticisms of yourself or others that isn't particularly constructive or insightful. In short, the ego's messages may sound an awful lot like the kind of negative mental chatter that sometimes seems to run on a continuous loop in our minds.

It's more likely to be intuition if the messages you're receiving say things like:

Go ahead; keep moving forward even if you don't know what the result will be. Have trust. It may look scary, but take the chance.

Even if, when you do move forward, you're not immediately

"successful" in the traditional, ego-based sense, there may be something else at play. You may end up encountering someone or something new that will positively impact your personal or business life. You might be getting exceptional practice for something that will come to you later on. Or maybe you're being saved from what lies down the path you were steered away from by your intuition.

It does take trust. You may well never know the reason your intuition kicked in. But the truth is that listening to intuition works out more often than not, especially when you are unattached to the outcome. You can't say, "Okay intuition; I'm going to do what you say. It just better work out great!" That's not trust. That's not the way it works.

And finally, just because you get a message to do something, don't abandon common sense. Sometimes intuition is there to wake you up or communicate through symbolism. Not all messages come through in black and white, neatly packaged and with written instructions. It takes time and practice to develop your intuition. The more you work at it, though, the easier it gets to decipher the messages.

The exercises here and the content of the next few chapters are focused on developing the core concept that in order to create divinely, you need to tap into your connection with your higher power, learn to listen to it, and trust the outcome.

In Real Life

When confronted with a decision, ask for spirit's guidance. Put a hand over your heart, shut your eyes, and just listen. See what comes up. Even if nothing comes to mind immediately, you're opening the channel. Pay attention as you go about your activities during the day. See what unexpected ideas or events transpire in response to your opening up to guidance.

Start checking in regularly with your inner guidance. What's it telling you? Examine what you're hearing and ask where it seems to be coming from. A place of fear? Is the message you're getting control- or achievement-based? If so, that's the ego talking. Or is it love- and compassion-based? That's coming from your soul, your Authentic Self, your higher power.

Block out a ten-minute period during each workday. During that time, set the intention to get guidance on one step to move you forward in your life. Just listen until something comes up. It may be right away, it may take nine of the minutes; don't rush it. When the message does come, run it through your rational mind. If nothing is out of line, follow it.

The exercises here offer you a plan for developing your intuition around a current situation or challenge.

Access the exercises through the membership site at
http://tiny.cc/scl-member

18. Soul Lessons

These concepts are preparing you to tackle leadership with a whole new perspective, one of divine understanding. The point is to bring you to the realization that all things are perfect. They may not always seem that way on the surface, but our job is to dig deeper, to understand ourselves and thus the world better, and to embrace the challenges and joys awaiting us. You might think of this process as fostering a type of extreme ownership of your life—one based on the soul-level of existence.

What you'll learn in this chapter is the final, profound step in fully accepting yourself, what you've been through, and what you're going through. It's my personal favorite, and I and many of the people I've worked with on it have found it deep and even a little intense. So as you read and work through it, keep an open mind.

To start, picture one person in your life who you associate with major heartache.

All of us usually have at least one person with whom we're really upset with on some level. Someone we wish had never entered our lives. When we think of them, we cringe.

Who is that for you? Your ex? A friend who you feel betrayed you? Someone who bullied you when you were young? A parent who still nags you about pointless stuff and never gives you a moment's peace? (Go ahead, you can admit it, I won't tell anyone!)

Whoever it is, bring a picture of them to mind.

Next, imagine that before your human life started, your soul was in a kind of heaven getting ready for your human experience.

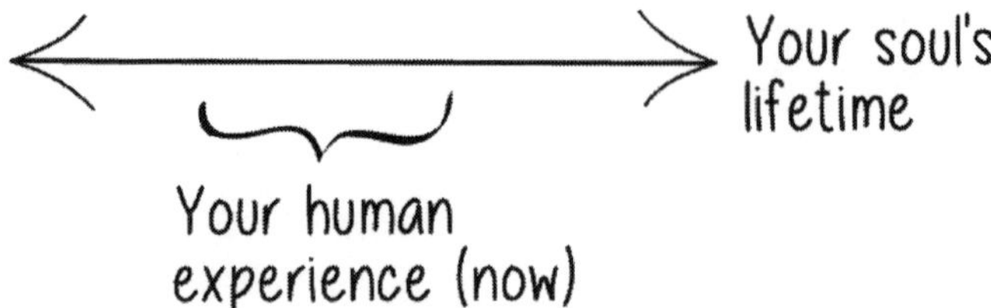

Picture it up there, looking down on the Earth, preparing to descend, and knowing that it has certain lessons to learn in order to evolve.

In fact, there's one lesson in particular—a doozy of a lesson—that will bring about great learning. But in order to receive it, to take it in and make it a part of your essence, you realize that your human form will have to go through intense suffering.

Now sitting next to you in this heaven there's another soul, a kind of best friend to your soul. You two would do anything for each other. Maybe there's no such thing as time in this heavenly realm, but if there were you could say that you've known each other forever, and you share true love in the most divine sense.

So it's the most natural thing in the universe for your soul to ask a favor of the soul sitting next to you. But from our vantage point here on Earth it seems like a very strange "favor" to ask.

"Will you," says your soul to the other, "take the form of the person on Earth who will be a source of suffering for me? Can you take that on? Can you bring me heartache and pain? Will you be the one I can trust to bring me what I need, while I'm in human form, in order for me to learn what I need to learn?"

And a wave of the purest, most intense love rolls over you from the other soul, and you know it has accepted this duty. It is an act of supreme love, for although the last thing this soul would ever want to do would be to bring pain into your existence, it realizes how important learning a critical lesson is for you, and so it accepts the role of "teacher" for your journey.

There really was no question that it would do this, because it loves you, and that's what souls do.

What this means is that this terrible person in your life, and the horrible thing you went through, is there because on some level you asked it to be there.

That's a life-changing shift in perspective. Because if that's true, how you can you ever judge that person? Or judge anything that you go through? Or judge yourself?

Now apply this perspective to other parts of your life.

What if it's true that you choose your parents? Your soul chose them because you needed them to be who they were to move you forward on the soul level. You chose your family, your teachers, your children . . . And they chose you. From this understanding, there's no one to blame. There's only love—acts of love from soul to soul, in a cosmic interplay of souls evolving.

If you can embrace this understanding, forgiveness and acceptance begin to come to you easily, naturally. You drop all the old stories that you've been carrying around, the ones that talk about "fair" and "unfair" things that happen. You let go of your judgments of yourself and others. Insecurities and outmoded beliefs fall away. You free yourself to engage with life in exciting new ways. Your confidence and trust in the universe and all that happens to you grow to form a foundation that supports your evolution. You start to connect with people, old and new, in ways you never thought were possible.

This shift in thinking means that everything is truly an expression of learning, evolution, and love.

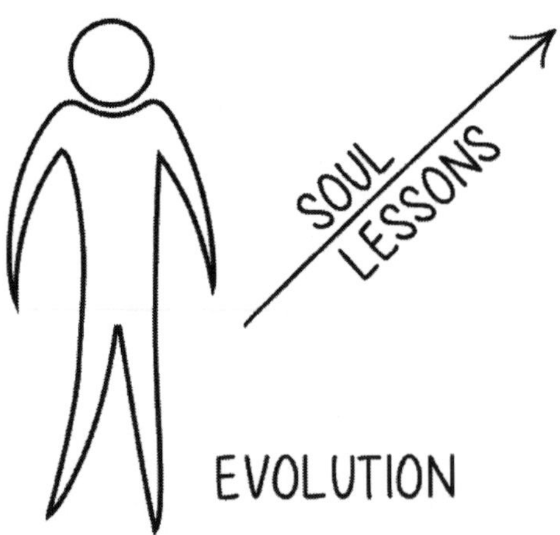

Love comes in so many different forms, and we can mistake it for many other things, especially when it comes in the form of hardship and suffering.

In fact, these soul lessons are why we are here on earth.

Each and every single person's purpose is the same – it's to evolve on the soul level.

Your purpose doesn't have to do with making money, building a business, or even having a family.

It's to personally evolve. And what brings up those evolutionary opportunities? Creating.

Where else do you normally get pushed? Do you feel uncomfortable? Where else does it take trust and courage to move forward?

It's when you are building something.

So drop all those old beliefs about purpose. Just focus on living the most conscious life you can. Then you'll get true fulfillment, and most likely create more than you could have ever imagined. Because that's the way the universe works.

If you adopted this way of thinking, how would your perspective on things change? How would you respond to new situations that in the past you would have considered difficult, even debilitating? You would start asking yourself questions like, "What is the lesson in this situation?" "How can I evolve through this?" Your attitude would shift from one of blaming and projecting to one of introspection, compassion, learning, and forgiveness.

I'll tell you where I saw this modeled to me, and it struck home.

During one of the Freedom to Choose Project workshops I mentioned earlier, the husband and wife team in charge of the program, Bonnie and David Paul, were addressing us before the event started. They said that some people knew they had applied for a sizeable grant that would really allow the program to expand. Unfortunately they didn't win it.

For a split second, you could see the disappointment on Bonnie's face. Then she simply said, "Well, it looks like that wasn't for our highest good. Spirit must have something better in store for us."

It amazed me that she could "work her process" in that very second. Yes, she's human and had some attachment to getting a big grant to fund her organization. And that was her reaction. Yes she had the awareness and chose another response. One of learning and acceptance. She instead chose to trust that the universe had something better up its sleeve; not getting the grant was not worth getting down about. What was important was moving on with the work, for her, for the other students, and for the inmates.

As a leader, you no doubt find yourself in many different types of situations. The goal of sharing these tools with you as you move into Soul-Centered Leadership is for you to become unshakeable. When others go into self-doubt, withdrawal, and anger, you stay centered and look for learning and opportunity. Now that develops an engaged, motivated workforce.

I now know that by going through the lawsuit with my first business partner, I learned about setting boundaries, believing in myself, and trusting my intuition. Now I look at that situation through the lens of having chosen to have that relationship "happen" to me, on some divine level. I am now grateful that it happened. I made it through, and I learned those lessons. Because I would never have become the powerful businessperson I am today if I hadn't learned those lessons. And there was no other way for me to truly embrace that learning.

It's the part of the journey that makes me a hero today.

In Real Life

The past few chapters have helped you realize the lessons to be learned in whatever's happening in your life. This skill is about moving into acceptance, compassion, and finally gratitude for your path.

Have you just figured out the lesson in something? Take a second and imagine your soul choosing to go through that. What was your soul's thought process? Can you thank yourself right now?

When someone or something new comes into your life, keep in mind they may be there to teach you a lesson. Be proactive; see what lesson they are there to give you. The quicker you learn the lesson, the quicker it will pass and you will be open for any abundance the universe may have for you.

The exercises for this chapter have to do with moving into gratitude and complete acceptance for what you have been through and are going through.

Access the exercises through the membership site at http://tiny.cc/scl-member

19. Surrender

There's a popular misconception today that somewhere out there there's a special purpose or passion that you need to find, and when you do find it you'll be happy every single day. On top of that, you'll help millions of people and make an incredible amount of money. If you haven't found your purpose / passion yet, look harder, because everyone has one!

Hopefully you understand by now that this isn't true. We don't have a magical-one-thing-we-will-do-for-the-rest-of-our-life-make-a-ton-of-money-help-a-lot-of-people-and-live-happily-ever-after. This is an ego-based dream that's easy to sell in our complex modern world. It's like a quest for the Holy Grail, the one thing that will solve all of your problems—all of life's intricacies and challenges and suffering—in one fell swoop. Wouldn't that be nice? No need to cultivate patience or dedication or compassion . . . Just find that one thing and live happily ever after.

You just learned about Soul Lessons in the previous chapter. Along our journey—our hero's journey—we face challenges that may seem contrary to our best interests. But one of the things we must remember, understand and embrace is the fact that the universe knows what it is doing. It puts people, challenges, opportunities, and everything in our lives at just the right time. And it's up to us, with our free will, to decide what we do with those situations.

> ***When we can look to see the message being given to us, lean into it, and enter the flow, beautiful things happen.***

There's a word for entering with, going with, the flow. The word may seem a little strange and, again, contrary to what you think is best for you.

That word is *surrender.*

The first time I was told this I thought to myself *surrender! What? I never surrender. This isn't for me. I'm a fighter. I get things done. Surrender is for the weak.*

You can see I was thinking of "surrender" in terms of fighting. When you surrender, I was thinking, you give up to the other force. And this is true to a certain extent. The definition of surrender is *to agree to stop fighting, hiding, resisting, etc., because you know that you will not win or succeed.* When you surrender you give your control to someone else. If that "someone else" happens to be someone you're actually fighting, either physically or emotionally, surrender is not a particularly appealing option.

But imagine surrendering to a force that *unequivocally* has your best interests at heart.

Imagine surrendering to a force of pure love: your higher power.

An all-knowing, all-loving universe, which only exists to help you evolve far more effectively than your brain and ego can get you to do on their own. Surrendering to this force is about what we've been discovering all along: letting go of all your control, surrendering your ego, and placing it in the hands of a divine force that loves you more than you can ever understand.

Yeah, that may be a good force to surrender to.

What surrender means is quitting your resistance to following the path of the universe. It means accepting the gift your higher power is offering you.

In such a case, anything less than surrender is you thinking you know better than the universe.

Now, I know you're smart, but you're not that smart.

Surrender doesn't mean giving up, and it doesn't mean stopping your engagement with the world around you. Don't think that this is for the lazy or unambitious. It's the opposite. Surrender means diving into the flow of life. It means embracing and acting upon whatever comes your way. It means completely accepting all of it as a divine message.

I'm sure you've heard of situations in which people had to hit rock-bottom in their struggles before truly finding faith and trust in the universe. This is because it took that moment of despair, of true suffering, for them to let go of the ego, and for the ego to let go of trying to control everything. Individuals who find themselves in this situation feel they have no choice but to surrender. Hopefully you can get to the place where you surrender before things get that bad; there's no reason to wait! You don't have to suffer before surrendering to life.

An Everyday Practice

Every day my spiritual practice includes looking at what's going on in my life and making sense of the clues the universe is giving me. In the areas where I'm experiencing stress and resistance, I usually find things to which I feel attached, whether that's outcomes or people or an emotional state. Often I am typically trying to control something about that situation as well.

Once I understand this I begin a process of reorientation in the direction the universe is guiding me. First I go into greater detail. What does this situation involve? Where is my ego at play in it? What are my options for more constructive action? Am I on a track that I should get off of? Maybe I'm holding onto a timeline that is unrealistic, and arbitrary? Or maybe I'm making something much more difficult than it has to be?

Then I look at where opportunities may be presenting themselves. Maybe it's someone I just met or something I recently heard about. Things pop up at the right time. Because I'm mindful and intentional about it, I have much better recognition and awareness of how that fits in with my life.

You can see how the tools that we've been discussing up till now fuel this process. Understanding the role of ego, refusing to play the role of victim, seeking out possibilities for change, letting go of the things that get in the way, following our intuition . . . As we learn more about these tools and engage them in our everyday lives, we not only open up existing paths that we hadn't paid attention to before—we actually *create new ones* as well. These paths unfold in our lives, sometimes in the most unexpected ways.

Let me share a few examples of surrender at work in my own life.

Around the time I started speaking professionally, Entrepreneurs Organization, the largest organization of entrepreneurs in the world, was holding its global leadership conferences in Panama and the Philippines. They were the perfect profile audience for my message, so I asked for inner guidance on how to move forward. I knew there was an opportunity there, but I was uncertain what it was and how to take advantage of it. What I got back from my intuition was "Why not just reach out to them?"

Two phone calls, two e-mails and one month later I was on the agenda for both events.

Speakers who had been in the business for years were blown away. They wanted to know: What had I done to get booked? I told them the truth: I simply picked up the phone and asked.

They had never thought of that. Let this be a reminder, too, that the gifts of the intuition don't need to come shrouded in clouds of mystery in order to be of use; sometimes they show up as simple, so-obvious-that-I-didn't-think-of-it ideas. Because how often do we make things so much more complicated than they are?

Another example: In a chance encounter I met Greg Horowitt, who runs The Rainforest Project: The Secret to Building the Next Silicon Valley. It turns out he needed a speaker on self-forgiveness. A few weeks later, I was speaking at Stanford University to innovation experts and government representatives from all over the world.

Both of these speaking examples involved me acting on spontaneous impulses. Had I been preoccupied with other concerns and agendas or wrapped up in other mental drama, I might very well have resisted, rejected or simply ignored them. But because I was open, because I had surrendered to the path the universe was laying out for me, I seized them. I don't say this to brag, only to point out that the very same tools are within you even as you read this. It's just a matter of training yourself and using them, and I hope that's what you're learning how to do from this book.

I find timing also has a lot to do with things. Often for me, what my intuition will say is, "That's a great idea Mike; just not right now." My intuition also helps me decide when something *doesn't* need to be done right now, to give it time. Sometimes the best way to sort out when to do something involves getting in touch with your intuition. Planning and strategizing are very important, but you can also spend a lot of time stressing about something that may never happen.

What if this employee quits? What if this large client leaves? What if they sue us?

There are so many things that *might* happen. Spending time and energy on them may not be at all productive. You're giving your energy up to "what-if's" when it could be more constructively used to press on. After all, the fact is that if one of those things *does* happen, you'll deal with it. You'll accept without judgment, and take it from there. Remember, too, that if what you're worried about does come about, maybe—just maybe—it's happening to help something better open up.

Living in the Flow

Think of your life as water flowing downhill. It's trying to travel the shortest route. Surrendering is letting it do precisely this.

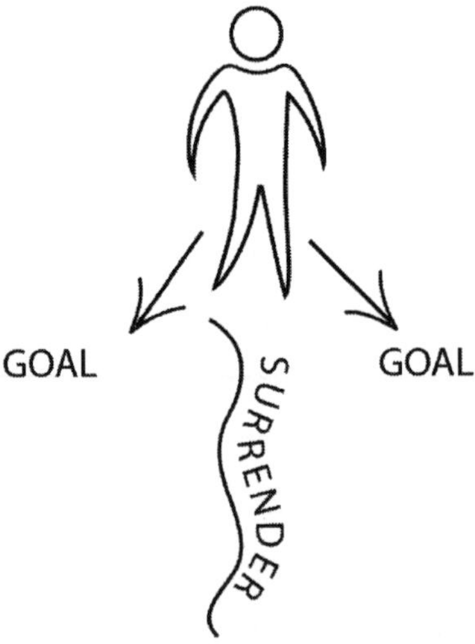

If you try to redirect water, it moves in your chosen direction for a short distance then returns to its original course and heads downhill. Water's powerful stuff when it's flowing. You could even say it's got a mind of its own. So wouldn't it just be easier to go with, to accept the flow of the water instead of exerting your will on it—and succeeding for a little while before the flow takes charge again? Which approach sounds more exhausting? Keep in mind that you're ultimately going to end up in the same place anyway . . .

Consider the possibility that every single thing that happens in your life is for your greatest good. This means that every divorce, lawsuit, argument, crime, failure—and success—is something that the universe created for your evolution.

In my own situation, I can now see that if I hadn't gone through my divorce, I wouldn't have learned about relationships and myself the way I did. I experienced a much more rapid—and intense!—personal evolution based on that experience, and I am extremely grateful for it. Of course, when I was going through it, it felt traumatic, difficult . . . brutal. I resisted it every step of the way for a while.

What if back then I had been able to follow my own advice now and had surrendered to it? What if I had been able to see even then that it was a profound opportunity to learn and evolve? Hindsight is 20/20, right? But I know I would've been a lot more graceful. And humble. And I probably would've gotten through it without half the suffering I felt.

But then I would be a different person than I am today. And I guess the universe knew that the me back then needed to undergo that experience in order to learn some vital lessons.

The same applies to my relationship with my former business partner. He assaulting me was the turning point for my own personal transformation. In a way, it focused several of the instabilities and insecurities I had around my business and my life. By working my way through that experience I learned or reinforced most of the concepts we've talked about in this book. Self-forgiveness, reflection, compassion for myself and others . . . All of these showed me the way through the bad feelings as well as the lawsuit.

Remember Viktor Frankl and the idea of reframing? That's what we're doing now, on the most powerful level available. The divine level. For my own part, I'm actually in a state of gratitude for the situations that felt so devastating at the time. The way I see it, the universe loves me (and all of us) so much that those experiences were gifts provided for me for my evolution.

Always keep in mind that the universe never gives you anything you can't handle. If it looks difficult, it's there to make you stronger.

You always have that free will choice. When something happens, you can resist it, blame others, and feel sorry for yourself. Or you can accept what is happening and respond with leadership and love.

Surrender involves letting go. We surrender our negative judgments of ourselves and others. We lay down our anxieties and fears and pick up trust instead. We give up our need to control everything that happens to us (as if we could do that anyway). And we know that when we clear our inner paths of all the clutter that's been clogging them, we make room for new joys, surprises, and challenges to manifest as we continue on our way.

In Real Life

Anytime you run into a negative situation, scan yourself for your ego. What are you holding onto? What are you trying to force? Then let it all go. Just be present and in the flow.

When something happens, pretend it's a clue to a greater meaning. If it's a signpost, where might it be pointing?

The exercises in this chapter give you a roadmap to surrendering in your current situations.

Access the exercises through the membership site at http://tiny.cc/scl-member.

20. Service

When's the last time you did something for someone just for the sake of making their life better? You weren't concerned with getting paid, receiving a pat on the back, or anything else. And as you were performing the act, a deep sense of fulfillment washed over you.

That's called being of service to someone else. As you learn and integrate the skills in this book into your life as a leader, and as you move more into harmony with your Authentic Self, you're going to naturally shift into a service mindset. It's going to give you the sense of accomplishment and joy that you might be missing and craving right now in your life.

> ***Being of service, or in service, is an elevated way of doing business that centers on earning through giving. It's the path to true fulfillment.***

It's one of the most elevated states you can achieve. Service reminds us that we are all connected, that our nature is that of being loving and kind. The more you practice the tools you've learned above, the more natural a service mindset becomes. In fact, the service mindset helps strengthen the principles we've been discussing. Through service you practice being unattached to outcomes. You're present, and you connect with others. You set your ego aside and surrender to your role in the process of helping others. And the more you move into a loving and compassionate relationship with yourself, the more you are driven to give back to. It's a true positive feedback loop: the more you evolve, the more you look to be of service. And the more you are of service, the more you evolve.

Shift to a Service Mindset

How do you bring these ideas into your business life?

The answer is simple: *Shape your entire business to be an act of service.* Make your business another way in which your higher power works through you. Create value for others in and through your business. It's an act of trust that you will be rewarded for the value you are giving out. The same holds true for your employees, vendors, and stakeholders; they too will benefit from the business's service mindset. Just be sure that you aren't trying to be of service simply to reap rewards; for some reason that expectation interferes with the process—rewards never seem to come as easily when you're attached to them.

A friend of mine, Drew Louis, owns Del Toro Loan Servicing. When investors make loans to others, they process them, help with the setup, send out statements, and so on. Drew was having issues with his company. His employees weren't very engaged, he had high turnover, and his growth was stalling. People just weren't that excited about coming into work every day and helping process loans.

When he began searching for a solution to these problems, he found that on a deep level he was of great service to his customers. The people who were taking out loans through his company were sending their kids to college, buying their dream home, and taking vacations they'd been planning for years. None of these things would have been possible without his services. What it boiled down to was this: Drew's company was giving its customers freedom.

Drew embraced this idea and made it part of his company's DNA. He got clear on the value he was bringing. He presented this to his company, and embedded it into everything they did. The attitude of *service*, of helping people manifest what they wanted in their lives, began to infuse all the processes that kept the company going, all the interactions between team members and clients.

People who didn't get it left the company. New people were added only if they got excited about how the mission of the company—being of service. The result? Turnover dropped and revenue, profits, and customer satisfaction all skyrocketed.

All this cost Drew *zero* money; it simply took a shift in mindset.

Realizing Worth

Being of service doesn't mean giving away your services. In fact, it can mean just the opposite. There's power in charging what your goods or services are worth. It may seem ironic, but charging what your services are worth actually gives them value in the minds of your clients, and this in turn can increase the impact they get from them. By under-charging, you are doing a disservice to your organization, your customers, your employees, and of course yourself. Not to mention that practically speaking, no business will be able to call itself that for long if it gives away its goods and services.

Charging what things are worth can also be part of your evolution, as I see many people have self-limiting beliefs that they should not charge a fee, or not charge consummate to the value they are giving. Remember how your soul's evolution is learning soul-lessons and you grow and create? This is a prime example. If you have fear and resistance to this, that's a clue there's room for growth.

That said, many companies do give value – for free or heavily discounted – as part of their strategy. Instead of advertising or aggressive sales, they see where they can add value to their customers in order to form relationships and learn if they and their customers can both benefit from an engagement. Or, they serve groups who don't have the funds to normally purchase their offerings for the full price.

When sales are lagging, most companies do more of the same ineffective marketing or have their sales teams make even more cold-calls. Instead of doing more of what isn't working, why not find where you can add value to someone and work from there instead?

Adopt your Business Model

My first company sold expensive, complex, enterprise business software systems. Instead of trying to talk a company into spending $250,000 with us, we would offer them a free or low-cost project where we would spend time determining their exact requirements and building a business case before embarking on a year-long project with them.

When someone comes to my current organization and wants one-on-one coaching, we offer a session at no-charge to see if there is a fit between the coach and the client. It's not just about the coach's ability; it's also about how they and the client work together. Whatever the answer is, the client gets value out of the session. Each and every one of my coaches loves this approach and enjoys the process. After all, they are doing what they do because they live to see the change in people, and it's important for them to know they can facilitate that process.

Here are a few places where adopting a service mindset will change the way you do business:

- **Sales** – Is your sales force not effective? Look at your sales processes; are they truly showing value to the prospect?
- **Marketing** – Is your marketing and advertising adding to your prospect's life? Or are you just telling them to buy your product?
- **Customer Retention** – Companies that are service-minded have customers who are raving fans; so much so that they keep their customers forever; the customers keep on buying and they're so happy with the service that they spread the word, and so becomes a major source of referrals.
- **Employee Recruitment** – Your mission and purpose should be well stated, and the people who are on board with making it happen actually seek *you* out to join your organization.
- **Employee Engagement and Retention** – Employees are so energized by their contribution to the mission that they are naturally engaged, loyal—and stay forever.
- **Stakeholder Support** – Other groups associated with your company—for example, suppliers, investors, referral partners, and the local community—often know of and support your mission, and they will go out of their way to help you thrive.

Soul-Centered Leadership engages the tools that allow you to interact with everyone, in service, from the Authentic Self, the place of love. Once you open up to that flow, the divine pays it back with untold gifts.

In Real Life

Before any interaction – with employees, prospects, customers, suppliers—anyone, really—set an intention that you are going to see how to truly serve them.

In the Exercises section, you will evaluate different areas of your life and see how you can shift to a service mindset.

Access the exercises through the membership site at http://tiny.cc/scl-member

21. Intentions and Inner Knowing

Goals, goals, goals. It seems like everyone's always telling us how we need to set more and better goals. They offer their strategies on how to set them, how to track them, and how to complete them.

The thing is, goals don't work for me. Every time I've set a strategic life goal, whether it's to make a certain amount of money in a year, grow my business to a certain size, or achieve whatever it was I wanted to achieve, it never truly gets me to where I wanted to go. And this is coming from someone who's achieved a lot. I have two masters' degrees and I've lived in six countries, played semi-pro basketball, and am on my fourth company. So it's not like I haven't gotten anything done. But none of those came as a result of a specific goal. Now I simply don't set goals.

I know—I can almost hear every coach and manager out there freaking out. How, they ask, can you move forward in life without goals?

Okay, so maybe I'm being a little dramatic . . . Let me explain. Goals, by definition, are ego based. It's what our ego wants us to do. And that's fine, because remember: the ego isn't bad. We just don't want the ego to be the driver; we want our ego to work in service to our Authentic Self.

Look at your life goals. Are any of them about having more money? The size of your business? Buying a certain car / house / boat? Marrying a certain type of person? Having your kids achieve something specific?

That's ego my friend. That's you trying to control the universe. That's a very human thing to do, of course. There's no shame in it. Until you understand how to go about things differently, trying to control it seems like the only option you've got. But what you're learning in this book is how to let go of that control and trust that the universe knows better than you do. You're giving yourself another way.

Soul-Centered Leaders use inner knowing to guide where they're going, and then use ego and goals to support the journey.

When I've had great success, both for myself in the material world and when providing value to others, it's been because I was following an inner knowing.

When I signed up for my MBA, I didn't say that my goal was to get my master's degree in business. I just knew it was the right thing to do at that time. And earning that degree was easy and graceful. In fact, I got an assistantship for which the school covered my tuition and room and board, as well as paying me to work at the Small Business Administration part time, so I got compensated while acquiring essential real-life experience.

Starting my first company was natural. I listened to what the market and the universe were telling me. I was profitable and cash-flow positive from the beginning. The opportunity came to me, I followed it, and as for long as I stayed in that flow, we flourished. During that time, I was focused on my people and on creating great customer relationships. I was making great money and I had a wonderful team providing excellent service and value. I was in a place of service before even knowing that concept. I was also having loads of fun. I was on numerous fastest-growing company lists, both locally and nationwide, and I won awards for my leadership.

Then, my ego took over.

How did it manifest itself? Here's what it sounded like: I have to do more! I have to have more! My new goal was to be the top company in my industry, and I set other goals in place around this: achieving a certain ranking in the top companies, a certain number of sales by a certain date, and so on. All focused on the external goal of being the best.

When I reflect on the reasons why I decided I had to do this, I realize now that I wanted to show the world how important I was. In my own way I was trying to prove my worth through my business success. I can still feel the ego that went along with that goal. I wanted to crush all the other competitors. I hated them all. I planned. I schemed. I obsessed. I hired coaches and consultants. I poached superstars from other businesses. I poured tons of money into sales and marketing.

I, I, I. It was all about me.

Guess how the universe responded? None of the sales and marketing yielded the results I wanted. In fact, we stopped growing. Profits shrunk to a fraction of what they had been. I had personnel problems, lawsuits, difficult clients, cash flow issues—none of which I'd ever had before. No matter what I did, I couldn't push through to the next level. All because I was ego driven instead of being in service to my clients and employees.

Looking back at the business situation as it was then, I can see that staying in the flow would have meant I had to be comfortable with running a company that might have stopped growing. My ego definitely didn't want this, because it would've meant I'd have to give up an identity that I'd put so much of my self-worth into. Namely, I had to be successful no matter what, to keep growing, to conquer my competitors and rise to the top of the heap.

If I had followed my Authentic Self and went with what the universe was giving me, I could have kept it the same size, made an enormous amount of money, had a great time, and had the space to focus on other things in my life.

Of course, I have to remind myself not to judge that time, and to forgive myself when I do. In retrospect, anyway, it's clear to me that the universe was giving me a much-needed lesson in surrender, flow, and intuition. And I'm beyond thankful for it.

Ahhh, universe. You got me again!

The Proper Use of Goals

And what did I learn about goals from that experience? One of the things I took away from it was the proper relationship between my intuition and goals. What I do these days is listen to and follow my inner knowing—and create goals, measures, and boundaries to support it. In this context, goals play a supportive role to messages from my Authentic Self.

For example, the idea for this book came to me, and as I thought about it, more and more concepts and themes for it started flowing into my brain. I was really excited about this, and I sat down to write it . . . three times. But each time I found I was forcing it. It took me a little while to realize that it wasn't the right time yet, and I was just wasting energy. So I held off and asked for guidance. Some time passed, and then one day, all of a sudden, I knew it was the right time to write the book. Every cell in my body was giving me that message, and the universe cleared my schedule and put me in an ideal situation (see the chapter on The Story about This Book).

Of course, even though it was the right time I still needed discipline to get the writing done. My ego played tricks on me and it was all too easy to find reasons not to write. So I did what most writers have to do: I set goals in place to support my writing. No appointments before lunch to save the morning for writing, when I write best. No heavy breakfasts. Workouts in the afternoon. Writing at least 90 minutes every day. And so on.

In short, I used the organizational and goal-setting powers of the ego in service of my Authentic Self.

Now it's your turn. Look at your life goals. Really reflect: where are they coming from? Is it from a place of service, value, and knowing? Or are they goals because you feel you should do them? Maybe they're not even yours! Maybe they were suggested by a mentor, business coach, partner, or investor. There's never any shortage of people asking you to do things or wanting to dispense (often conflicting) advice.

What would it look like instead if you were guided by a higher power?

Goals versus Intentions

Goals can be the enemy of surrender when not utilized correctly.

> ***Goals can make you deaf to guidance, so it's important you are clear on your path before setting them.***

Intentions are different. Here are few of the major differences between them:

- A goal is about the future. An intention is about the present.
- A goal is often something you can't control. An intention is about how you will be.
- A goal focuses on the outcome. An intention focuses on the process.
- A goal is about winning or losing. An intention is about how you are going to live.

Say you and your sales team are headed into an initial sales meeting. A common goal might be to close the deal. But during the meeting you're so attached to the goal's outcome that you don't take time to listen and understand the prospects needs. Maybe there isn't a good fit, but you push forward anyway and force a close in order to reach your goal.

As your relationship unfolds the fact that your offering isn't right for them becomes more and more apparent. This ends up creating a problem relationship, one that isn't profitable and which creates issues in your organization and in the marketplace.

An alternative to setting a goal before the meeting is setting an intention with your team: We will be present, truly listen to the prospect, and in service to seeing if there is a match between their need and our offering. Let's say that with this new approach, during the meeting you begin to understand that your service isn't right for the prospect, so you communicate this to them. They respect and appreciate that, and in return, they refer you to another, larger prospect.

Always keep in mind, when you are in the flow, present, connected, and unattached—that's when the universe rewards you.

Connect to your inner knowing to determine your direction. Use goals for what needs to get done in support of your inner knowing. Start setting intentions before meetings and conversations. And don't worry – if you move from goals to following your inner knowing and intentions, you will end up much more successful, all while freeing up more room and energy in your life.

Listen, Trust, and Follow

Let the universe tell you your direction. When you're in a state of surrender, unattached to any particular outcome, that direction will be revealed to you. You'll experience an inner knowing, an impulse to create something. Maybe it's a company, a book, or a blog. Possibly even a relationship or a family.

But when you try to do it the other way around and tell the universe what your goal is, it has a habit of laughing at you.

This too is part of your Hero's Journey: learning that lesson. The universe is bigger than you and me and everyone else put together, incomprehensibly vast and rich and unknowable. Most of all it's there to support you. Why would you go against that?

Make it easy on yourself and make it easy on the universe. Give yourself over to the divine. Start listening . . . and flow.

What will the results of this approach look like as they unfold in everyday life?

Let me share another personal observation. I was at a speakers' conference, and a few of us were talking over lunch. One of the members asked me what my strategic business goals were. I thought about this for a moment, then said,

"I don't have any."

He looked at me, a little surprised, and so I started to explain to him and the others present what I meant. I explained that, sure, I have things I'm working on, like this book. But what will I do after I write and market it? Some ideas are present, though I'm sure that the right course of action will present itself when it's ready. I don't have to know now. I just have to be ready, listen, trust, and act when I experience a knowing about what to do. That's what surrender is.

If you want to know what my personal goals are, I only have two (and they're actually the same one stated two different ways...) To deepen in my spiritual practices and engage in surrender to a greater level. All day, every day. Because when I do that, everything else falls into place.

Of course, these aren't goals as much as intentions. There's no "winning" or "losing," no targets to meet, no business to grow. Only myself. And you can't put a value on that. We're all priceless.

That's what this whole book is leading up to. It's about you learning these techniques. To do this you need to read the book, go through the exercises, and take part in the online community.

When you do these things, you'll be engaging in the process of clearing out the cluttered pathways of your consciousness, slowing yourself down and connecting to your soul—so that you can hear the messages from your Authentic Self and follow their guidance.

This power that's available to you can't be compared to anything else. And what it has in store for you is greater than anything you've ever experienced or imagined.

In Real Life

Intentions are very powerful when set before interactions—for example, before phone calls, meetings, composing e-mails and even writing proposals. Some simple but powerful intentions include:

- My intention is to communicate clearly and authentically
- My intention is to be of service to this person
- My intention is to be calm and listen to my inner guidance

Start to be aware of when your ego is in play and starts making goals. Normally this will be in a competitive situation or around a group of your peers. At such times, stay centered and set an intention to have your Authentic Self provide you with a course of action.

Where are you encountering resistance in your life, especially around goals? Take a minute to see what moving from insecurities and resistance and into love and flow would look like.

As you follow your intuition and inner guidance, give yourself credit, pat yourself on the back. It takes courage and connection to do what you're doing.

The exercises for this chapter are particularly powerful, as the shift from ego-based goals to inner knowing is a truly transformational process.

Access the exercises through the membership site at http://tiny.cc/scl-member

22. Self-Worth

Author and teacher Caroline Myss says that we aren't born with self-esteem. It's something we have to build up ourselves. Do you see how all of these tools we've been learning along the way here are doing just that?

Much of conscious evolution is building up this self-confidence and trust. You live for yourself instead of worrying about the approval of others. You can finally let go, surrender, and move into acceptance, and in doing so, you truly embrace your power.

Soul-Centered Leaders take the principles we've been working with throughout this book and infuse their practice of leadership with them. Look at how insecurities lead to poor leadership and management:

- Micromanagement is when someone doesn't trust others, which is a projection of them not trusting themselves.
- Lack of transparency is really lack of trust around being vulnerable. It's an expression of a need to hide.
- Gossip comes from an individual putting another down in order to feel better about themselves.
- Not listening to feedback from employees reflects the "Independence Curse," where an individual feels compelled to show that they are in charge and know it all.
- Failing to delegate may indicate that an individual fears change and is afraid to take on the challenges and responsibilities involved in higher-level activities.
- Lack of respect and talking down to others means the person isn't happy with themselves.

All of these behaviors also serve as defense mechanisms for people who are afraid of getting "found out"—because they feel like frauds.

When we're insecure, we make decisions based on fear. Those decisions usually don't turn out well. Fear doesn't tend to have people move forward; rather it inclines people to either stay where they are, afraid of making any moves, or to retreat.

In my own case, I brought on my first business partner not because I needed his expertise, but because I was scared and lonely. It was difficult for me to handle the growth and responsibility of a rapidly growing company, and at that time I didn't have the tools to manage myself. I wanted someone with whom I could go through the process of business ownership. I wanted companionship. I didn't think I was ready or developed enough to go it alone, so I gave the first person who came along some equity and it ended with him assaulting me and a lawsuit. I made the decision to take someone on because of my own insecurities, not out of any solid reason. And look how that turned out for me!

Years later, when I was selling that same company, I engaged in months of negotiations. As we started to wrap up our negotiations, both parties were so invested and attached to having the deal go through that even though the universe gave me clear signals not to do the deal, I did it anyway. It ended up being an expensive mess, and lawyers had to get involved to straighten it out.

So I got those two lessons handed to me on a silver platter by the universe: don't make decisions based on fear, and listen to your intuition. I was learning the principles of Soul-Centered Leadership—the hard way.

Realize what Truly Matters

On the other side of the coin, when I have felt connected to my Authentic Self and intuition, I have brought great things into the world.

For example, in one of my companies we went through a few mediocre office managers. Finally my operations officer and I decided that the office manager role was one we needed to fill with someone who could do a truly stellar job. We agreed that we would keep interviewing until we found the right person. So we set aside an entire day and thoroughly interviewed seven people in a row.

The fifth person in that day was a young man, twenty-five years old, named Russell. My intuition told me immediately that he was the right person. I said as much to my COO; she was a little skeptical since he didn't have the traditional skills we were looking for, but I remained convinced. We still interviewed the remaining two candidates. After this my feeling was still strong about Russell, and I knew the choice had been made.

Over the next six years, the young man blossomed. Russell was the person I could always rely on. He did whatever needed to be done, and in return I mentored him and kept him on his upward path. Sometimes my executive team got worried I was giving him too much, but he came through each and every time. He quickly climbed our ladder and earned everyone's respect. Even though he was in his late twenties, I watched him blossom into one of our top technical people—on a team where the others were between forty-five and fifty-five.

A year after I sold the business, Russell went to work for a much larger company. In less than three years there—now only in his mid-thirties—he proved himself and earned a VP position. Not long after his promotion I had dinner with him, and he told me, "Michael, I want to thank you. I got the new position because of what you taught me."

"Because I taught you the software industry?"

He shook his head. "No. That was something, but it's mainly because you had confidence in me. You supported me the whole way. You taught me emotional intelligence and soft skills. I know how to deal with people. It's amazing to me how others don't. It's what sets me apart."

Hearing that—and working with Russell in general while witnessing his growth—is one of the highlights of my entire business career.

Your technical ability and drive may get you started in your work life, but it's what Russell talked about that's the real difference maker. Yet the skills he was using, the skills that landed him a VP position and continued success, can only be mastered by someone who is practicing them on themselves.

Have Faith - In Yourself

You have tremendous power, but you can't access it until you're comfortable with and accept yourself.

What happened in the past doesn't matter. Quit judging it. Quit judging yourself.

What will happen in the future doesn't matter. Stop worrying about it.

Be present. Be strong now. Remember your potential and just make the highest-level decision available to you right now. That's all you can do. And that's when you will feel true fulfillment.

Remember, you're in school. This is all just a lesson. The universe is helping you learn.

There's one self-forgiveness affirmation that instantly connects you to your divine nature:
I forgive myself for ever thinking that I know better than God.

Of course, you can substitute in higher power, the universe, or whatever fits for you for that last bit.

Because it's so true. All this higher-level stuff is going on around you, but somehow you think that you're smarter than the universe?

Ha!

Okay, okay. I'll let you off the hook. The truth is, you don't really think you're smarter than the universe. You've just forgotten that the universe is there to support you. You don't have to go it alone. You don't have to try to fix or create or solve everything by yourself. All you need to do is remember that you're not alone.

Surrender to your path, your journey. Have faith.

Here are two more overarching affirmations that cover just about everything:

I am unconditionally worthy.
I am inherently loveable.

What this means is that just by being a soul you already have everything you need, and are everything you need to be. You are already perfect. You don't need to do anything to become worthy of love and affection and be accepted. You are already worthy.

You don't need to have anything to be loved. You already are. Here's one more:

I am loved more than I can ever fathom.

The universe is love. And there's some kind of higher power out there, which you are a part of in some pure way. Pure love, pure compassion.

Just be open to that. It's available to you at any time.

Right now.

And right now.

And two weeks ago. And tomorrow.

When you stop living out of the need to receive the love and acceptance of others, you can truly be yourself.

Think about it. The universe is waiting for you to step up and use your talents. The universe is waiting for you to be yourself. How hard can that be?

"Your gifts were not given to be lost in your own unworthiness." –Marc Darrow

In Real Life

Did you just do something out of insecurity? Remember that it's natural and normal. Forgive yourself. Be compassionate with yourself. Now, how can you take ownership for what you did and show up as a Soul-Centered Leader?

Need some confidence? Remember, we aren't meant to be perfect, and no one expects that of us. Go inside and ask for inner guidance. Get present. Work from there.

Everyone goes through self-doubt. Courage is moving forward in spite of that. What's a small step you can take to move forward?

Are you accepting praise from others? The next time someone gives you a compliment, simply look them in the eyes and say, "Thank You." No equivocating, no brushing it aside. Just "thank you."

Recall the times in your life when you've been at your best, doing great things, serving people, feeling good. I don't mean climbing Mt. Everest or breaking two million in sales—though if you have happened to have accomplished these things, put them on your list! But I'm really talking about leading with compassion, forgiving yourself and others, feeling at peace with who you are, serving others selflessly, or in general just getting done what needs to get done in a spirit of strength and self-respect. Once you've got some of these moments in mind, ask yourself: If I took on these things in the past, can't I simply continue along this path? Can't I build on these successes until I'm practicing Soul-Centered Leadership—for myself and others—all the time? What's stopping me?

On the membership site, in addition to the exercises, there is a Confidence Journal, which is a simple and easy way to gain true confidence and self-esteem by recognizing your own power. It's something I developed when I was running two of my software companies, working ten-plus-hour days. At the end of the day I was exhausted, but I felt like I hadn't accomplished anything and this caused me to get really down on myself. After two weeks of writing in this journal nightly, I was energized, full of power, and getting more done than ever before. Start your own Confidence Journal online.

Access the exercises through the membership site at http://tiny.cc/scl-member

23. Your Groove

In the Soul Lessons chapter you learned about what your soul's purpose is. Now that you've learned about surrender, service, and other spiritual practices, it's time to utilize them to give you a greater sense of direction and focus in your everyday life.

While I brought up the fact that there isn't this perfect purpose or passion that needs to be divinely figured out, that doesn't mean that you're already placing yourself in the position to be of greatest service while being fulfilled and growing all at the same time. Life is a process. Sometimes you'll be engaged in one activity more than another, and then things will switch up again. I call this finding your groove.

Your groove is temporary. That is, as you grow and evolve, your groove will change. But in general you'll know when you're in your groove for a number of reasons.

First, when you're in your groove, you provide great value to the world. You can feel and see the benefit others get from your work. When you're in your groove you're in one of the best places to be in greatest service to the world.

You'll also sense when you're in your groove because it's really, really fun and fulfilling. You may have to overcome some resistance to get there, but once you're in, it's very enjoyable. Ironically, sometimes it's so great that your ego says, "Wow, this is so awesome, but there's no way I can make a living at it. So I won't even entertain that possibility." That, of course, is a self-limiting belief. But you know how to deal with that now!

Another element of the groove is that it builds on your past, as well as your positive qualities. In other words, you don't have to suddenly learn a whole new skill set just to get into your groove. It's something that you "slip" into. You don't have to swim against the tide to get into it.

On this note, people sometimes get nervous about finding their groove. For example, a salesperson may ask, "What if my groove is doing accounting? I hate accounting!"

Fortunately, it doesn't work that way. The universe didn't give you the gifts you have not to use them for humanity's gain! Your groove is fun for you. And there are elements of it that you'll already be prepared for. The universe also has been always prepping you for something greater; this is why your past experiences and current skills factor into your groove. Of course, as mentioned above, your groove will change as you do, so you will have at least a few over the course of your life.

And at certain points in your life (normally short and transitional times) you may not be able to get into any groove. The path of the Hero's Journey forces you to learn soul-lessons along the way. The Hero often has one character issue that they need to overcome in order to complete their mission. That may be the case for you, especially during these times of change. Maybe you have to overcome an issue of worthiness. Perhaps you're too wrapped up in your ego, and this keeps you out of synch with your groove. Maybe you're developing your feminine energy and need to release your attachment to making a certain amount of money or living a certain kind of life. Or maybe you are still developing your masculine energy and need to charge boldly forward, really putting yourself out there, and leap into your groove.

Put Yourself in a Place to Shine

One of my friends started an internet marketing company. We were having a conversation, and he said, "Michael, my life sucks. I really don't enjoy work anymore."

"Why not?" I asked.

"I love being in front of clients and designing solutions, but now, since we've grown, all I do is handle operational issues. I have to be involved in the accounting, hiring, everything. It's just not fun."

"I don't understand. Why don't you head up the sales division and hire someone else to be the President and run the company?"

He looked perplexed. "How would I do that? I'm the owner!"

"That's exactly why you can do it!"

He was caught in a self-limiting belief that he had to be the one who handled all of these things, despite the fact that his lack of interest in them and the time it took away from more pressing things was hurting his company. Another factor was that his ego also wanted him to have the title of President (when he also could have taken the role and title of CEO and still hired a president). He was definitely not in his groove.

Changing Grooves

When I look back at my life, I see that my groove has certainly changed. When I was thirteen I taught myself to program in the basement of our house. I would spend hours in front of our Apple II; I was so comfortable behind the keyboard in my own little world. That lasted for years. It taught me critical thinking, it gave me confidence, and it allowed me to have a great safe space.

These experiences in turn propelled me into university and then on to my first job, where I used those skills to make a name for myself. Then, as I continued to learn about the software industry, I became a salesperson and a leader. It took a while, but after a lot of learning and growth built upon the foundation that had been laid down earlier in life, leadership became my groove. And I continued in that vein with my own companies.

After that, the next stage of my life had to do with my personal transformation and this lead to my current groove: writing, teaching, and speaking.

So I've had at least three big grooves in my life, not to mention many small ones like basketball, spending time with orphans in Mexico volunteering, and cooking. And I certainly didn't go right from one groove to another; there were these transition times, and these required hard work to achieve enough mastery for me to feel comfortable in those roles and understand how to act in service to others.

Remember, your nature is to create, and leadership is a great strength and gift. It's possibly the greatest skill needed for creation. Since you're reading this book, there's a good chance that creating something big and bold and leading others is your groove. Or maybe you're in a leadership position yet you feel it's out of your groove. You can develop comfort and mastery in leadership, in fact that's a natural progression, and that's what my programs are for.

Whatever your groove is, just like most everything else in this book, you have to grow and evolve to both find and live it. It's up to you to take ownership and find and create it. When you do, you'll feel incredible.

There is no *In Real Life* section in this chapter. Instead, go to the Exercises to work a process for finding your groove.

**Note: this is a very big subject that many people want clarity on. There is a good process in the Exercises section, though I've run this as an online course before with group coaching, and it's been very successful. If you have an interest in taking part in a more in-depth course to really work your process around finding your groove, send a note to info@executivejoy.com. If enough people are interested, I'll run it again.

24. Soul-Centered Leadership

You are a leader.

You're not a leader because you happen to own a business, have a certain title, or are in a leadership position.

You are a leader because you choose to be a leader. And choosing to become a Soul-Centered Leader is the most powerful choice you can make.

Unknown, wild, crazy and wonderful things are possible for you. Opportunities so massive you aren't even aware of them. That's why you need to embrace yourself as a leader. And fortunately, right *now* you have all the qualities you'll ever need to ascend and elevate. You just have to activate them. My goal in writing this book has been to help you do just that.

Fast-forward with me to a time when you've embraced what you've been practicing here. Picture walking into a room, centered, present, in the flow. You're so comfortable with yourself that you naturally connect with everyone, and they are drawn to you. As issues arise, you observe and absorb the information, and solutions flow to you easily and naturally. People are amazed by your calmness, kind directness, and creativity.

They want to head in the same direction you're going. They just don't know how to get started.

These are the people you need to serve, first and foremost as an example. At a time when worldwide employee engagement is at 13%, the way to galvanize people you work with, especially millennials and the younger generation, is to connect with them. And there's no deeper level of connection than on the soul-level.

These individuals are thirsty to follow someone who's ahead of them on the path, because the path is scary and requires courage, inner strength, and trust. It's a path best travelled with others.

It's the path of enlightenment.

Whether they realize it right away or not, people *want* to be on that path. They want to be moved, to become what they *know* they can become. People will be on your team because they believe in you. They see your noble qualities and feel intuitively that you can help them on their way—just as others have helped you, me and everyone who walks the path of life. So *shine*. Inspire. Lead. If you do, they will never leave your side and you will teach them to be their very best.

Leadership is Influence

The world is in a delicate position. On the one hand, things have never been better. People are living longer and healthier lives than ever before. Violent crime rates are at all-time lows in almost every place in the world. Technology connects us in ways we couldn't even imagine just twenty years ago. Yet when you watch, listen to, or read the news, it seems like it could all go up in smoke at any time. Just a few people with misdirected anger can disrupt entire countries.

How can we effect change in the world? What can we do to contribute to a better world? Enter politics? Sure, a few politicians can influence change, but only in certain situations, and often only for brief periods of time. Other public figures can have influence as well, though these are few and far between.

Lasting change comes from the people who build, influence and create. Service is the currency of the soul. With Soul-Centered Leadership you are learning how to create sustainable greatness for all involved. How to effect change in the world? Become a business leader. As a society we are always generating innovation after innovation, changing lives and the world around us. As this kind of leader you are positioned to serve the world by leading at the forefront of positive change.

But wherever you find yourself, whether a business leader, a teacher, an artist—the principles of Soul-Centered Leadership will help you drive change for the better in your own life and the lives of those around you.

It's time for you to embrace your leadership. Get comfortable with the fact that you are a leader.

That in itself will at times feel uncomfortable. Most likely when you find yourself in a new leadership position, you will try to fall back to a place you're familiar with, someplace where you're comfortable. Those self-limiting beliefs and the voice of ego will be strong; they'll tempt you to take what seems to be the path of least resistance—but that's really just a state of stagnation. The sooner you can free yourself from them the better. Not only is it okay to be a leader, to accept the fact that you're in charge—it's necessary.

Embrace Leadership

I was once training with the Navy Seals at a special event, and I asked them what they felt was the biggest inaccuracy about war movies. What was the one thing that they absolutely get wrong in Hollywood?

They told me that when you see the general on the front lines leading the charge, that would never happen. In fact, if their commander were ever in the line of fire, they would knock him over the head and take him to safety.

I was surprised. Didn't they want their leader to be on the front lines, risking his neck alongside them? Absolutely not. They have all the strategies and battle plans in their head. If they get wounded or killed, the whole platoon is at risk. They're commander for a reason. They've trained for this. Their second in command doesn't know the orders, what the overall strategy is, and what they've said to the other troops. Other people are there to shoot guns, drive the tanks and move forward. What they need to do is lead.

In your organization, you're that commander. Your people are looking to you for the battle plan. It's great to connect and listen to everyone, from the people on the front line on back. And no one is better than anyone else. You're all worthy souls. Everyone has to understand their role and their value.

Your value is the vision, strategy, and leadership. You should not be doing HR, finance, or cold calls. If you are, you're doing your organization a disservice. If you're not delegating, you're not fulfilling your role. In a way, you're playing it safe.

Your Job is to Lead

Once, at the end of a basketball season, one of my teammates and I were parting ways for the summer holidays. He asked what my plans were for the offseason. I let him know about the trips I was planning to take and he got upset with me. He told me how important it was to train and get better in the offseason.

"It's our job as teammates," he said, "to do the absolute best we can in each of our roles. That's what makes a strong team."

That statement really sank in. While collaboration is important, it's only as effective as the skills of the individuals on the team. Everyone should be masters of their craft.

And your craft is leadership. Leadership is the number one aspect that determines the success of a business; it shapes everything else at the company. How often do you work on your leadership abilities? How much training do you get? Do you reflect on what's working and not working, and sharing best-practices? Are you training your team, especially the high-potentials?

You know that leadership isn't just a matter of having a title or directing people or achieving a certain sales target. It's about becoming who you are, and showing other people who they can be. That's why this book and a consistent practice, are necessary for you to continue to grow and evolve your most important skill.

Always remember that you are a creator. Your job here, on this Earth, is to create. Your ego tries to stop you because it doesn't feel safe leaving its comfort zone. It has devised clever strategies and tricks to hold you back. But there's always more to the picture, and more to you.

As you build yourself into a Soul-Centered Leader, always keep in mind that you have the one tool that works in every single situation – your connection with your higher power.

Slow down. Go into your quiet, special place. Connect with it. Ask for guidance. Receive. Then act. You've seen how you can affect the world. You've had tastes of your soul-centered power.

Keep going.

You have everything you need right here. Read this book again.

Do the exercises. Participate in the online community. Create your destiny. Choose to be special. Get out of the way and let the divine do the rest.

What the universe has in store for you is more than you can ever imagine.

You just have to ask it.

Go forward.

Trust.

Accept.

Surrender.

Lead.

And Love.

In Real Life

Whenever you encounter a new situation—for example, when you walk into a room or someone comes to you with an issue, where are the leadership opportunities? Ask yourself, "How would a Soul-Centered Leader act right now?"

Are people who work for you or around you not engaged? Why? How are you showing up that might attribute to that? What shift can you make to take total ownership of yourself and be an example of someone fully engaged?

In every moment, ask yourself; "How can I live up to my potential? What's the highest-level decision I can make at this time?"

Are you experiencing resistance? What's going on with your ego? Shift your focus onto your Authentic Self and remember your core essence is a creator.

Take a minute and go into silence and just listen. What's your intuition telling you to do?

Go through the exercises section to identify where you aren't fully showing up as a Soul-Centered Leader and what different choices you can make to get there.

Also included is a bonus Soul-Centered Leadership affirmation, specifically created to anchor the learning into your everyday life.

Access the exercises through the membership site at
http://tiny.cc/scl-member

Part IV - The Soul-Centered Leadership Box – Putting It All Together

Now that you have this set of tools, you might be thinking, "Wow, I've learned so much. How do I remember everything? How do I put all this stuff into action in my everyday life?"

Introducing the Soul-Centered Leadership Box. It's a way for you to take any issue and follow the nine steps in service to working with it in the most conscious way possible. This may not be something you use on each and every issue, but when something important comes up that you want to work with, sit down and work the box. It's designed to be a comprehensive system encapsulating everything you've learned. Because sometimes you have to bring out the big guns!

A friend and collaborator, Natalie, read an early copy of this book. Her first comments on the box were just so-so. Then the next day I got an e-mail with the subject line, I was wrong... Natalie went on to say:

The chart is phenomenal. I'm walking through it and every single question has lifted the fog. I cannot tell you how much this has lifted my funk, lifted my spirit and transformed the way I'm viewing my work. . . Best questions ever asked. BAR NONE. Fantastic work.

Reading further into what Natalie said, this specific process may not be the most simple out there, yet it is powerful. So first review it without pressure to just get a feel for it. Give it a little time to sink in. While nine steps may seem like a lot, you're actually working through a matrix, and you don't have to memorize anything to get started. Everything should already feel at least a little familiar from what you've read in this book. That's all you need. It's really just a helpful way to put everything you've learned to work.

Note that because of space limitations in the printed book the font on the charts may seem a little small, but in the membership site there are printable versions along with worksheets that accompany this chapter.

The three columns across the top are Awareness, Response, and Compassion, which you've already learned as the ARC system, and which you have been working through in the exercises.

The three rows are the levels in which you will be working.

- The first level is External, which encompasses your actions and everything outside of your inner world. These are your actions and behaviors.
- The second level is Internal: your thoughts, feelings, and beliefs—the mental and emotional level.
- The third level, and the deepest, is your Spiritual, or soul-level.

Awareness	Response	Compassion	
External Awareness / What's the Situation?	External Response / Behaviors	External Compassion with Others, Forgiveness	External / Behaviors
Internal Awareness on the Mental and Emotional level	Internal Response on the Mental and Emotional level	Internal Compassion on the Mental and Emotional level, Self-Forgiveness	Internal / Mental & Emotional
Spiritual Awareness on the Soul-Level	Spiritual Response on the Soul-Level	Spiritual Compassion, Gratitude, Evolution	Spiritual

We can refer to the use of this comprehensive tool as "walking the box," because you start on the upper-left, and snake through the box, as you can see in the following diagram.

And remember as you read what follows: You don't have to recall any of these details. You can download worksheets to guide the process, as well as a printable version of the entire box.

Awareness	Response	Compassion	
What's the issue being addressed?	What agreements and commitments do you need, with yourself and others, here? Taking full ownership, and concentrating only on what you can control, what's your response? What's your highest-level action, your potential, here?	Forgive the other person. Go through the action with compassion, while keeping your energy in a neutral to positive state.	External / Behaviors
Start with some mindfulness. How are you reacting? What are the: -Identities -Attachments -Judgments -Projections -Disappointments What do you need to own here to move forward? What self-limiting beliefs may be at work here? What is your fear? Can you let go of anything *right now?* Are you in true integrity?	What does it look like without judgments or attachment (from acceptance?) What can you let go of? What does surrender look like in regard to this issue? How can you be of service? How can you overcome your fear and resistance? What does authenticity and vulnerability look like here? Do you need some balance with your masculine / feminine? How do you show up in true integrity?	Forgive yourself for any and all judgments you were holding against yourself. Understand your truth. Would an affirmation help you?	Internal / Emotional & Mental Level
Are you out of balance with your masculine / feminine? How's the relationship with yourself here? What could the soul-level lesson be here? Why might your soul have chosen this to happen?	How can you reframe this issue? How is this part of your Hero's Journey? What clues is the universe giving you about this? What's your intuition telling you about this? What does surrender look like in this situation?	Have gratitude for this lesson. Remember, it's a gift, and you've handled it in a conscious way. You've just evolved your soul.	Spiritual

Here is each step explained in detail. Directly after each section is a real-life example of me running the process on myself, step-by-step.

While there are a number of questions, you need not answer all of them. Some go quite deep and involve advanced skills, so if a few don't resonate, either skip them or go back to the relevant chapter, reread it, and do the exercises. Everything contained in this process here has been covered in a prior chapter.

Step 1 – External Awareness / What's the Situation?

The entire process starts with you choosing an issue you would like to address.

It could be anything that's either a current situation or something more long term that you want to explore or change.

Example

The issue: I contacted someone who I thought would be a good fit to help me work on this book as a marketing assistant. I thought they would be cost-effective, and I believe they would have done a good job. This individual expressed interest, but didn't get back to me after I reached out a few times. I was getting frustrated.

Step 2 – Internal Awareness on the Mental and Emotional level

This is where you start to utilize the tools you have learned.

Awareness starts with mindfulness. Find somewhere quiet to get dialed into what's really happening with you. Go into a short meditation, or at least sit with yourself for a few moments.

Now, remember, everything is about you. It's not about the other person, or whatever else is going on. No one can make you feel anything. Move out of victim mode and own 100% of your internal state right now. Be careful to not judge yourself while going through this stage in particular. You are simply making observations in service to your growth. It's actually a very courageous act.

- What's present within you? What emotions and feelings?

  Remember, it's okay to have those emotions and feelings. Feel them and accept them.

- What identities are you playing into?

  Remember, an identity is something you identify with / as, and you use it to justify unhealthy behavior. Examples: Hey I can be late; I'm the boss aren't I? / That's what my dad did, so why can't I? / I'm an entrepreneur, so I don't have to be respectful. / Women aren't supposed to speak up. / That's how people from my region are.

Common identities include husband, wife, boss, employee, son, daughter, entrepreneur, man, woman, specific religions, specific nationalities, cities, regions, etc.

- What attachments do you have to an outcome?

  Remember, an attachment is a desire for something to work out in a specific way, with your happiness contingent on it.

- What disappointment do you have from an implied agreement?

  Remember, sometimes we make assumptions based on things that weren't communicated, and then we get let down. We thought someone was going to act in a certain way or do something, yet it was never explicitly discussed, and now there is disappointment.

- • What are the projections?

  Remember, a projection is when what we see in the outside world is a reflection of how we see ourselves. If something outside of you is upsetting you, how does that relate to your relationship with yourself? Are you secretly doing that very same thing, and are you worried that you'll get caught? Or do you try so hard to not be that way that you judge others who are?

- What are you judging?

  Remember, a judgment is where you are assigning the positive or negative charge to the situation or person. The only true fact is that "it is," that the event happened.

- What self-limiting beliefs are in play here? What story are you telling yourself? What subconscious beliefs are holding you back? How are you self-creating this upset, and where does it come from?
- Where are you procrastinating? Where are you experiencing resistance?
- • What are your fears around this situation?
- Where are you out of integrity? Where have you not kept your word...to others or to yourself?

You might be able to get a head start on things. Is there anything that is easy for you to let go of right now? Something not serving you that's easy to move forward without?

Once again, take 100% ownership, and have self-compassion. That combination is unstoppable.

Example

I noticed myself getting upset. I slowed down and checked in with myself;

- I was attached to them getting back to me
- I was attached to them being the right person for me
- I had judged them as a bad person
- I was disappointed yet we didn't have any explicit agreements with response times
- I had a self-limiting belief that if someone doesn't jump for me, that means I'm unimportant and not worthy
- I was too masculine-energy heavy; I wanted to control and make this work
- My projection was that I have fear about being not reliable myself, because that will mean I am not valuable and therefore not worthy
- I do have some fear—that they'll be too expensive, or that this is a great option and it will get away, and I won't find someone else (I realize these are mostly unrealistic fears, though most of the time that's how they show up)

Wow! So much going on with such a seemingly small issue.

Step 3 – Spiritual Awareness on the Soul-Level

Now you move from what you are feeling internally to what the universe and your higher power is telling you.

- Are your actions or approach overly masculine or feminine here?

  Remember, masculine energy is action-oriented, competitive, direct, risk-taking. Feminine is nurturing, collaborative, creative, and intuitive.

- How is your relationship with yourself right now?
- What could the soul lesson(s) be right now?
- Why might your soul have chosen for you to go through this?

  Those last two questions are by far the most important questions you can ever ask yourself.

  If the answer isn't clear, and in cases you won't know until later or maybe ever, then list several options, and let yourself know that something you can't see is at work here. Have trust and faith that it's all for your higher learning.

  In fact, whether an answer reveals itself to you or not, it's good to write down three to five possible answers. Often there is more than one lesson. Even if it isn't time for you to know what it is for certain, you are opening yourself up to the fact that this is a learning experience.

The more times you go through this process, the quicker and more natural it gets.

Example

I was out of balance in my masculine and feminine energies. I was coming at it with a lot of masculine energy.

The relationship with myself was causing me stress and upset.

I was getting caught up in my attachment to something I couldn't control, which is their response (or in this case, lack of response).

My soul-level lesson is to accept and surrender. I'm teaching myself that through this situation.

Step 4 – Spiritual Response on the Soul-Level

Now that you know what's happening on all levels, it's time for you to start forming your response, starting with the Soul-Level and moving out.

- How can you reframe this issue?
- How is this part of your Hero's Journey?
- The universe is absolutely giving you clues. What are they? Spend some time contemplating what is happening and where the universe is pointing you.
- What paths are closing down?
- What paths are opening up?
- What actions are you doing that are getting negative feedback? What is simply not fun about the situation?
- What are actions that you've initially dismissed yet may actually be options?

  Remember, you don't have to commit to anything right now; just list different courses of action.

- What new person / opportunity has recently come into your life?
- What is your ego drawn to?
- What is your Authentic Self drawn to? What is your intuition telling you?

  Remember, it may not make total sense right now, or it may be uncomfortable or unexpected. Another strategy for tapping into this is to set an intention at bedtime to receive guidance from your higher power, sleep on it, and see what comes forward the next day.

- If you have any attachments, how might a new course of action work when you release that attachment?

  Think of the universe as having a sense of humor. When you are attached to something, the universe will, in its own way, laugh at your attachment. For example, if you are attached to making a certain amount of money, it may be so difficult to reach that exact goal, and then if you do reach it, it will be at a cost that makes life miserable.

- What would be a big, bold move that would take an incredible leap of faith and trust for you to move forward with?

  Often, when the universe has something massive and great in store for you, it will make you make a big move into the unknown.

- What would happen if you dropped all notion of control, and asked for the universe / your higher power to guide you? What would surrender look like in this situation?

In this section, the key question is "What would surrender look like?"

Example

I then chose to look at this situation as if it was the universe telling me that the individual in question wasn't the right person for me at this time. I settled on some affirmations and observations related to this decision:

There is so much more in store for me. The universe didn't want me to go this way, and it's giving me these clues.

My ego wanted that person to work for me. After checking in with myself, my Authentic Self and intuition knows that it is not the right person. In fact, I believe now that if I pursue this person and get them working for me, it will result in more difficulties down the road.

I realize I'm still a few weeks away from needing someone and that I don't even need to decide right now.

All that stress was self-created.

I do believe that by remaining open, with the intention for the right resource or resources to come into my life at the right time that I will be better served.

I let go of all control and trust that it will all work out.

Step 5 – Internal Response on the Mental and Emotional level

The Spiritual Response gives you a foundation for your Internal Response, which has to do with the emotional and mental levels.

- What are you choosing to let go of – identities, attachments, judgments, projections, self-limiting beliefs?
- List them out here, with the intention to move past them / heal them.
- What does the situation look like now, free of all ego-based thinking, as you look at it from a place of acceptance, neutrality, and divine guidance?
- What is a path of service in this situation? How can you give to others in a way that's free from attachment?
- How are you overcoming procrastination, fear, and resistance? How is this part of your evolution?
- How can you show up in a healthy, vulnerable way with full authenticity?
- How are you now acting with true integrity, with yourself and others?
- How are you bringing in more masculine / feminine energies to achieve more balance?
- As you let go of all that old stuff and embrace the divine, what shape is surrender taking?

Example

I addressed the situation with new understandings and affirmations:

I am letting go of the attachment to them getting back to me.

I am letting go of the attachment to having them be the "right person" for me.

I am letting go of the judgments I had around them being a bad person.

I take ownership of the fact that I didn't communicate a specific timetable for a response from them.

My truth is that I am worthy; that is not dependent on whether they get back to me or not.

I'm balancing out with more feminine energy of trust, faith, and nurturing (of myself); I realize this isn't a win / lose situation.

My internal response is to remember that the universe is a giving place, and that I'm always supported, and I trust that the right person, at the right price, right skill level, and right competencies, will come into my life just when they are supposed to.

I am letting go of attachments and everything else that is not serving me.

To be of highest service to myself, readers, and my new potential assistant for this book launch (whoever that may be), the best response is to surrender.

Step 6 – External Response / Behaviors

Now, formulate what specific actions you will take.

- How are you going taking 100% ownership, own your part in all of this, and step forward as a Soul-Centered Leader?
- How will you show up with true integrity, with specific, rock-solid agreements – with others and yourself?
- How can you live your potential, which is taking the highest-level action available to you, right now?

Example

Again, I made some decisions:

I'm going to wait until I really have a need for the resource. Then I'm going to get the word out and keep my eyes and ears open to opportunities and clues in order to see what greatness the universe has in store.

I'll keep neutrally evaluating options as they present themselves and be ready to move forward when it feels right to do so – which is a more feminine energy-based approach. (My energies in the past have been very masculine, so this is me consciously slowing down and not trying to control everything.)

Step 7 – External Compassion with Others, Forgiveness

Remember, everyone is doing what they think is the right thing to do at any given time, given the information they have.

- Are you taking things personally? Just let that go. It's only creating negativity in your life.
- Are you still holding onto any judgments about someone or something else? It's time to let that go as well.

Remember, people are going through their own Hero's Journey. It's not up to you to pity them or judge their process.

You don't have to necessarily like or agree with the person; you can love their spirit, their soul, their divine essence.

Get rid of your judgments and negativity, and simply love them.

Example

Regarding the non-responsive person, I can keep in mind that I don't know what's going on in their world. It's not up to me to judge their actions. It's up to me to accept them and the situation. Who knows; maybe they're sick, or a family member is. Or maybe they are just not ready for this responsibility. Maybe they have resistance and fear, and this situation is part of their soul-learning as well.

I'm actually helping them evolve by letting it go.

I forgive them for anything I'm holding against them. I love them as a soul and a divine being.

Step 8 – Internal Compassion on the Mental and Emotional level, Self-Forgiveness

Now that you've released the negativity regarding others, it's time to focus on yourself.

Looking back, how are you holding yourself in regard to this situation? What judgments do you have about yourself?

> Do you have any inner dialogue that says things like that was stupid, I should have known better, or I wasn't a good person? Just like other people, you were doing your absolute best and what you thought was right.

Hindsight can be so easy. Give yourself a break. Let yourself off the hook.

Forgive yourself. Understand your truth.

Say or write the following for each judgment you have against yourself.

I forgive myself for judging myself as... / I forgive myself for buying into the misbelief that...

My truth is...

> I forgive myself for judging myself as stupid. My truth is that I was doing the best I could, and I did a really great job overall. In addition, I'm very courageous for being self-aware and working the Soul-Centered Leadership box on this issue to heal at the deepest levels.

Go as deep as you can, explore every nook and cranny. This is true healing on the deepest level.

In fact, your version of "my truth is..." may turn into a powerful affirmation for you. Do you want to start integrating that into your life?

Build up that self-acceptance. After all, you're worth it.

And we need you at your best.

Example

I check in and do have some self-judgments. I am judging myself because I thought I should have known better by not having any judgments in the first place, not getting attached, and not surrendering the whole time.

Basically I was expecting myself to be perfect.

I forgive myself for buying into the misbelief that judging someone or something makes me a bad person.

I forgive myself for judging myself for judging someone else.

I forgive myself for buying into the misbelief that I am wrong for ever being attached to the outcome.

I forgive myself for judging myself as an unconscious person for not always being in surrender.

I forgive myself for judging myself as unworthy and unimportant.

I forgive myself for buying into the misbelief that someone else can determine my worthiness.

I forgive myself for holding standards of outer perfection against myself.

I forgive myself for thinking that I know better than God.

I forgive myself for judging my humanness.

My truth is I did a great job of recognizing that I had upset and judgments in this situation.

My truth is that I am human and that I am not a robot and that I will continue to, at times, judge people. And the truth is that I love myself just the same, whether I do that or not.

My truth is that I am a very powerful person and that I have the consciousness to see and heal these issues as they come up.

Step 9 – Spiritual Compassion, Gratitude, Evolution

Everything you went through is a gift. A gift of evolution.

And you were conscious enough to take it as such.

You are going through your Hero's Journey and were aware enough to accept it and bring love and compassion to yourself along the way. And because of that you evolved and moved through it quickly, with ease and grace.

- Can you even move into gratitude to the universe for giving you an opportunity to learn this lesson?

It takes a mighty, evolved being with a strong intention to learn these lessons. Your soul, and therefore all of humanity, has just moved forward.

Great job.

Example

To cap this process off for myself, my statement was;

I thank the universe for giving me this gift to see my unresolved issues, and thank myself for the courage, compassion, and consciousness to heal them and move forward.

How did it turn out?

As time went on, I knew the time to bring someone on was getting close. I was living in Zagreb, Croatia at the time (to see why, read about it in The Story about This Book), and out of nowhere, a young man named Marko reached out to me. He heard me speak at an event a few weeks before, was inspired, and asked if I could mentor him. He was looking for career advice.

I told him I don't normally mentor people; however I would have a coffee with him and see if I could give him any on-the-spot guidance. When we met, I was impressed. He was in his mid-20's, came from a difficult background, and had recently graduated. He had already started an organization called Motivation Up which was running events for millennials around the region to give them direction and inspiration.

He was bright, motivated, and above all coachable. So I asked if he was open to taking a position with me.

He said yes, absolutely, and he has since joined me and most likely when you join our community you'll run across him doing something. He's the exact right person, who came into my life at the exact right time, and he has been getting tremendous value out of our relationship as well.

That's what happens when you work your process, let go, and start trusting.

Now it's Your Turn

I really encourage you to take an issue you are dealing with and run it through the Soul-Centered Leadership box RIGHT NOW. It's something you have to experience to recognize how deep you can get with it.

Where do you go from here?

Warning: as you start your emotional and spiritual evolution, your ego will resist the changes. The messages you'll get will include: "This isn't having any effect on me," and "Okay, I've mastered this now." If you have a daily practice that includes doing these exercises for thirty of forty years, then yes, you might be approaching mastery. If that isn't the case...and let's be honest it isn't...then keep at it!

The ego is fighting for its life as it knows it. Remember the ego strives for comfort, control and security, all which you are threatening. So when you hear those messages from the ego, it's good – it means you're on track. Just be sure to reframe them right away.

In the membership site, you have access to a journal template to list your learnings as well as to catalogue your evolution and ascension (the Ascension Journal). Here you can write down what you've learned, what changes you have made in your life, how you are responding differently, and how you feel now that you are in a higher state of consciousness. It's something you can review when you're thinking you aren't getting much out of the practice.

And once again don't kid yourself. You can always learn and integrate these skills on a deeper level. Each one is a lifetime journey. No one ever lives in complete ownership or complete surrender all the time.

It's also not about making huge jumps. Keep in mind that you're changing long-standing habits. That means it's about small, consistent changes. If you can make a tiny change each day, one that moves the needle two percent, after a few weeks you'll see significant change. Just imagine a year or two forward. That's the road to transformation.

A few more hints:

- Don't take things too seriously; don't get attached to your rate of evolution, and stay the course.
- Experiment with what you are learning. Some of what you learn will be familiar, some will feel very new. That means it takes a few practice swings before you know how you want to hold the bat.

- Simply focus on living your potential. Don't tell others about the new you; show them. And if they ask, then tell them.

Before long you and the people around you will reap the benefits of another Soul-Centered Leader in the world.

Continue Your Training Online

As a companion to the book, go online and join a free 90-minute Virtual Training called ***3 Secrets to Transforming from Boss to Leader.***

In a short period of time you can learn some fast actionable strategies to motivate and inspire your team, shift your career into high gear and build something great.

Just go to http://tiny.cc/scl-course and sign-up now.

Appendix

The Story about this Book

There's an interesting story about how this book came to be.

In 2015, after living in San Diego for ten years, I became very unsettled. The universe started giving me signs that a change was coming. I had a few close circles of friends that fell away. Business became difficult. I couldn't find a groove anywhere in my life. I felt increasingly lonely and isolated. I knew something wasn't working, but I couldn't figure out what it was.

I looked harder at the clues. When did my mood change?

When I was travelling.

Whenever I had a trip scheduled, I would get excited. Then, while I was away I'd feel *alive* again. A few days after returning, I'd fall back into the funk.

The first half of my adult life I had lived in six countries. Mapping it out, every time I made a big move, my life took a big upturn. So now I finally realized: I had to make a move.

Where? When? How?

I fought this realization for a while. I tried to resist it, telling myself, "I can't really leave San Diego, can I? My friends and support group are here. It's comfortable. What am I getting myself into? What if I fail? There are too many unknowns."

After much internal deliberation, I decided to go all the way.

At the end of 2015 I sold all my things except for a few suitcases of clothes and necessities, and I became a nomad. As I write this, and probably as you read it, I live without a home.

As I was literally driving out of town, my car all packed up, I stopped by to do a podcast with Katy Bray, a psychic coach (listen to it here: http://www.katybray.com/podcast/ask-katy/ak011/). She helped me put things into perspective. I was at peace with the decision.

Then I listened to the audio book The Surrender Experiment by Michael Singer. It was the absolute right message for me at the absolute right time.

I surrendered. I let go. Life took me to Belize, Guatemala, Germany, Denmark, Croatia, Montenegro, Albania, and (of course) Little Rock, Arkansas. From staying at a $50,000 per week private tropical resort island for free, to a yoga retreat in Belize where I shared a bathroom with twenty others.

Spending a week or two in a city only to move on gets lonely. The second half of 2016 I had a few speaking engagements in Europe and wanted to make some connections that only come with staying in one place for a while. I chose Zagreb, Croatia, as I had a few contacts there and that's where my great grandparents are from.

I spend six months with that as my base. I finished the book, formed a support team, and spoke a lot. I learned an amazing amount; about myself, about different systems, about the effect war has on a region, as you may remember Croatia was at war with Serbia only 25 years ago.

I also taught the first Soul-Centered Leadership course, even before the book was finished. I didn't know how it was going to go over. We were going to cap the attendance at 20 students. Turns out we had such demand we raised it to 28. We had board members of banks to entrepreneurs to middle managers to people looking for a career change. And you know what? I had nothing to be worried about. This stuff is universal. It was a raging success. I even recorded the course and it's available by going to http://tiny.cc/sclcourse.

What an adventure. I loved and lost. Experienced high highs and low lows. Connected with old friends and made new ones. But the whole time I felt so free. So alive. And I still do.

You're reading the result of the trip. And I'm sure there's more to come.

The more I work on this book and this material, the more excited I get. I have an inner knowing about the change it will affect. It's a fun journey, one that certainly hasn't ended yet. And by reading this book it means you are part of my trip, and I'm part of yours.

Thanks for being my travel partner.

About Michael

R. Michael Anderson, M.B.A., M.A. specializes in teaching organizations, leaders, and individuals how to become even more successful through psychology, emotional intelligence, and spirituality.

By the age of thirty-five Michael had founded three international software companies, played semi-professional basketball (yes, he's really six-foot nine!), and partied at the Playboy Mansion—but he simply wasn't happy and thoroughly unfulfilled.

Hard drugs, alcohol, a divorce, and a nasty lawsuit brought him to a low point. A quest for change included earning a master's degree in Spiritual Psychology from the University of Santa Monica.

His unique background of real-life experience mixed with his world-class education allows his audiences to both learn and be entertained. An authentic and vulnerable speaker, attendees find him thought-provoking, inspirational, and unique.

Michael has taught leaders around the world, from Panama to the Philippines to Australia and Mexico, and has worked with a broad range of clients, including Microsoft, SAP, Stanford University, Vistage, Young Presidents Organization (YPO), and Entrepreneurs Organization (EO).

Made in the USA
Columbia, SC
26 March 2018